BRANDON SWIFT

Idea to Acquisition

Creating SaaS that Sells

First edition

ISBN: 979-8-53-220923-7

This book was professionally typeset on Reedsy.
Find out more at reedsy.com

Contents

Preface

There are so many books out there that can teach you to start a business. There are also a lot that teach you how to build a SaaS business - written by people more qualified than me.

Those books are great.

But this book is specifically about how to do what I've been doing for the past 10 years - building a bunch of smaller SaaS businesses, making money along the way as they grow and then selling them for a big (relatively speaking) payout at the end. Most books I've come across in this arena are about changing the world with your business and dedicating your life to major things, but SaaS doesn't have to be billion dollar companies and sleeping under desks as a startup. Instead of a 10 year journey to earn $100M, I propose you take a 12 month journey to earn $100k - but with more than one iron in the fire.

So this book won't teach you how to code like Mr. Robot or how to become a billionaire with your own space company. Instead, this is book is about a system that I use to build companies that people want to buy. I create a "business in a box" and sell it, complete with users and revenue - to the highest bidder.

You'll find some of the information is a little more instructional, but most of it is comprised of things I wish someone had told me when I started all this. My hope is to give people the tools to create marketable ideas, bring them to fruition and sell them for a profit. So for this book, I'll take you through my process of taking SaaS businesses from idea to acquisition.

Why start a SaaS platform?

What is SaaS?

SaaS (Software-as-a-Service) is a business model in which a company grants a license to use its software in exchange for a recurring fee. Generally, this fee is charged on a monthly, quarterly, or annual basis. Cloud-based SaaS provides numerous benefits for businesses and consumers over traditional software sales models. Businesses can service more customers with less overhead and customers can pay less up front to use software that's always available and up to date. This makes SaaS an ideal business model for startups with little to no funding and/or a small team.

From 2010 to the present, SaaS businesses have been popping up everywhere and have been gaining massive traction and attention. You see SaaS startups glamorized in movies and TV shows, generally highlighting the rare occurrences that many now believe are a necessary and expected part of starting a SaaS business.

It is assumed by many that, when you create a startup, you need a once-in-a-lifetime idea. Then you need to raise more money than you've ever seen - from a stranger in a suit. After that, customers come pouring in overnight, and the next thing you know you're the richest person in your hemisphere and keynote speaker at TechCrunch Disrupt.

Although it's happened more than once, these types of stories represent only a fraction of the complete story. Building big SaaS products takes a great idea, lots of funding, and a large team to be successful. Many companies who take this path still fail, spending millions of dollars and years of their lives on something that eventually gets shut down. The fact is over 90% of startups fail. If you've got a startup, those are the stakes, plain and simple.

Many fail because they aren't meeting a market need (ie. the idea sucks). Many because they give up (starting a business is tough – especially if you've never done it before). And many simply run out of money.

When you shoot for the moon the stakes are high. What movies and TV shows forget to mention is that there are plenty of other ways to approach building a SaaS startup that don't include sleeping under a desk, kowtowing to investors, and giving up your ability to have a life outside of work.

There's a middle ground where you can create products within a system that is designed to generate revenue and is easy to sell to investors. I've used the system in this book over the past 10 years to build and sell over 15 SaaS businesses, giving me the freedom to live by my own rules, create my own schedule, spend time with my family and be creative for a living. These weren't stories to make movies about – some of them sold for under $50k! The cool part is that the smaller apps only took a couple of months to take from idea to acquisition. What could you do with an extra $50k every few months from your side hustle?

When you're first starting, start small. You're probably not going to build the next Salesforce or Slack - and that's ok! While anything can happen with online businesses, and you could be pleasantly surprised, the goal of this book is to provide a repeatable system within which you can work.

We're not shooting for the moon here. We're trying to add an extra $100-200k a year to your salary (If you create 2 businesses per year), keeping the businesses that crush and selling those that don't work as well. That's right, you can even profit from your failures!

By the end of this book, you'll know the ins and outs of how to discover a great idea, validate it, build a product around it, perfect your pricing, create buzz, drive traffic, increase engagement, process payments, provide great customer support and position yourself strategically for acquisition. You don't need to know how to code, but if you do that gives you a huge advantage when it comes to cost savings.

You also don't need to quit your day job (although you might as you start earning recurring revenue from multiple sources). Everything discussed here can be done in an hour or two per day, right from your laptop.

Just like everything in life, you get what you pay for. The more time you invest in your business, the more valuable you'll be able to make it.

I recommend you read the entirety of this book before you start creating your first business, as there are many topics covered later on that you should also be aware of in the beginning.

3

Traditional SaaS vs. MicroSaaS

When most people think of SaaS, they imagine huge software companies with teams of developers, all with more money than they know what to do with. While there are definitely companies that fit that description, there are thousands of others with unique stories.

Many SaaS startups are small teams with only one or two people working for them. In fact, most of the biggest software companies start this way. Salesforce started, in 1999, as a team of four working out of a one-bedroom apartment in San Francisco. In 2006, a team of two launched the first version of Shopify after only two months of development.

The SaaS game is huge, and the playing field is vast. There are billions of dollars floating around and, for most people, even scraping a small piece off the side of a huge industry can be life-changing.

When we talk about traditional SaaS, we are generally referring to platforms like the aforementioned Salesforce and Shopify. They are self-standing solutions that businesses can pay to use. There are no other prerequisites.

These platforms generally solve complex problems. In this case, we're talking about building websites and optimizing your sales pipeline. Big platforms have tons of settings, a learning curve, and high development and support costs. They are also generally difficult to scale and require a solid team to keep them afloat.

But all SaaS doesn't have to be that big! Enter MicroSaaS. MicroSaaS is a term used to describe SaaS businesses that are smaller in nature, generally charging smaller fees, run by smaller teams, and are easy to use. MicroSaaS products will serve one or two specific functions and that's it.

A good example of a MicroSaaS would be StoreMapper.com. Instead of spending years on a major platform build like Salesforce, Tyler Tringas saw an opportunity with businesses that have multiple physical locations but no way to attractively display them on their website. In 2009, he built a simple tool that allowed store owners to easily create and embed a map of their locations on their website. That's it! That's all it did.

This wasn't a feature that most website builders had built-in, so there was a gap in the market that he could fill. Tyler ran StoreMapper by himself for a while, earning a living and traveling the world, and eventually sold his app to SureSwift Capital in 2017. Now Tyler has founded other apps and is an investor - without having to give up years of his life to a 9-to-5 or change the world to get there.

MicroSaaS just means you are building something that solves a single problem - maybe two at most. This allows you to become laser-focused on a solution that other platforms may overlook or see simply as "a feature". That additional attention to detail and understanding of the problem means you can solve it better and supplement other tools already in a business's toolkit.

When deciding what size project you should take on, there are pros and cons to both. I would suggest, however, if this is your first SaaS business, that you start with a MicroSaaS to get your feet wet.

Traditional SaaS solves big problems for customers and generates a lot of revenue, but it can take a really long time to build and get to market and generally requires a significant amount of funding. Mistakes can be much more costly going this route.

MicroSaaS is quicker to market and can be run by a single person, but generally is easier for competitors to copy and will make less revenue per customer.

Traditional SaaS Pros

- Solves Big, Difficult Problem
- Generates High Revenue
- Doesn't require other tools
- Generally vital to an organization
- High Barriers to Entry – competition will be slow to catch up

Traditional SaaS Cons

- Takes a long time to get to market
- Markets can be really competitive
- Expenses are high
- Learning Curve / Lots of Settings
- High Barriers to Entry – it's difficult for you to create

MicroSaaS Pros

- Quick to get to market
- Competition is lower
- Expenses are lower
- Simple / Easy to Use

- Low Barriers to Entry – it's easy for you to create

MicroSaaS Cons

- Lower barrier to entry for competitors
- Revenue per customer is lower
- Other platforms may be required to use it
- It may not be vital, but can still be justified
- Low Barriers to Entry – competition will come quickly

Whatever direction you choose, the sky's the limit and the same basic principles apply. If your price is lower, you'll have to put on more customers, but those customers will generally be easier and cheaper to acquire. If your price is higher, you'll need a platform with enough value to justify it, which can take time and lots of money to create.

Separate Your Income from Your Time

One of the most liberating aspects of creating a SaaS business for yourself is that you can separate your ability to earn from your time. This is the number one way to build wealth.

With most jobs, you either clock in and out, or you are expected to be present for 40+ hours every week to earn your pay. Even in what many would refer to as a "results-oriented environment", you can take the amount you are paid and divide it by the hours you are expected to work.

If you continue down this route, you will always have to work for your money. The only way to retire would be to stop earning and to live off of your investments (if you have any).

By separating your time from your ability to earn, you effectively free yourself of all limitations on your earning potential. As a human being, you can't trade 24 hours of your time every day for pay. You need rest and time off to survive.

As long as your time and your income are directly proportional to one another, you will have a hard limit on the amount of money you can earn at any given point in your career.

With SaaS, you have a product that is online and working for you 24/7 so you can earn while you sleep. This doesn't mean it won't require work, but it does mean that money you make isn't directly correlated with the time you spent making it and the work you do can be on a schedule you set for yourself.

Recurring, passive income

The reason SaaS businesses are so effective is their ability to generate recurring, passive income. Now, this isn't exactly true for all SaaS businesses. The larger you get, the less passive it all becomes. But for a team of one running a microSaaS, setting things up properly can mean creating a "money machine" that requires very little to maintain.

When you charge your customers the same amount of money every month, it's very easy to predict next month's revenue - this is what's known as recurring revenue. This predictability is how you can both work for yourself and feel financially secure.

Another great aspect of recurring revenue is that, if your business is growing every month, then your earnings stack month over month. Instead of calculating your income based on the time spent working, you instead look at your net new revenue plus your existing revenue, minus any customers who canceled (this is known as churn).

The formula below calculates monthly recurring revenue (MRR):

(NEW REV + CURRENT REV) - LOST REV = MRR

Let's look at a few examples of how one might earn $1,000,000 per year in different scenarios. We'll compare an hourly worker, a salaried worker, and a single-person team running a SaaS platform.

For the hourly worker making $20 per hour, they would have to work 50,000 hours per year. Unfortunately, there are only 8,760 hours in a year, so this isn't feasible.

For the salaried worker making $250k per year, well, they would have to make 3x their annual pay in bonuses and commissions to hit the target. That's pretty unlikely to happen regularly.

For the person running the SaaS from their basement which charges $50 per month, they would need just over 1600 customers. Considering over 4 billion people have access to the internet and there are over 125 million businesses worldwide, acquiring 1600 customers seems like an achievable goal, right?

But how long would it take to get there?

If they put on around 30 net new people per week - that's about 4-5 per day, that would take them about a year to get there. But the key here is that by the end of month one, they'd be bringing in $6k each month and building upon that as they grow - month two would be $12k, month three would be $18k, and so on...

So you see how much more realistic it is with a SaaS model to earn $1,000,000 per year than by working a traditional job. There are virtually no limits to your earning potential, you can work from anywhere and live the life you want.

But it's hard, right? Well, yeah, kind of.

I'll spend the rest of this book teaching you the tools and techniques I use to come up with business ideas, validate them and grow them into something you can sell. It's not all easy, but with a little determination and sticking to a process, you'll have all the info you need to go from idea to acquisition.

Tools You'll Need

If you want a system to create SaaS that sells, you'll need the right tools for the job. You don't need to spend a ton of money on them, but you need to live and die by them. The tools you use every day will determine how productive you can be and ultimately how successful your business becomes.

Project Management Tool

At the heart of any software development project, you'll find a project management tool. A project management tool will help you, your team, and the contractors you hire all stay on the same page every step of the way. There are many kinds of project management platforms and tools available, but I tend to lean toward kanban boards and iterating over 1 week periods.

Kanban boards are a way of laying out tasks in columns or "states", where each column generally represents a stage in the lifecycle of a task. Trello is a free platform where you can create Kanban boards and share them with your team. This is a great place to start if you don't already have a tool you prefer.

When you're deciding what columns to use on your board, think about the different stages a specific task may go through. A task can be a chore, a feature, a bugfix, or anything else. From the time it is added to the time it is completed, you need to be able to track the status of the task.

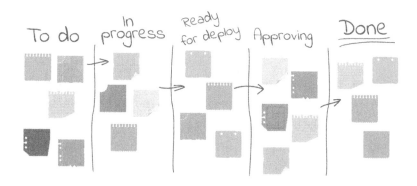

Kanban boards let you visually track your to-do list

Here are some "states" I like to use when tracking projects:

Current

This holds all the work for the current iteration and should be filled up each Friday afternoon for the following week.

Backlog

This holds tasks that have been added to an iteration but have not been completed by the end of the iteration. You generally want to try to keep this empty.

Icebox

The icebox holds tasks that you would like to complete but aren't pressing enough to be in the current iteration and haven't been scheduled before. This is where you put "nice-to-have" features requests.

Completed

This is where completed tasks go. You don't want to delete them once they're done since you may want to refer back to notes on the task at a later time.

When you add a task, phrase it in the form of a "user story". This allows you to convey a lot of information in a very short amount of text. For instance, if the task was to add a dropdown to the my account section that lets someone select their country, you could write it as "As a user, I'd like to be able to set my country from a dropdown from My Account". Similarly, if an admin feature needed to be added "As an admin, I'd like to be able to edit a user's country selection". By wording it this way, you paint a full picture that includes access level control, context, use case, and the actual feature itself.

Having a one-week iteration cycle means each week there are tasks to accomplish. You start them on Monday and finish them by Friday. You can decide how many tasks to assign a given week by scoring tasks by difficulty level.

I prefer to use Fibonacci numbers to score difficulty as there is no ceiling and it accounts for exponential complexity. This basically means if a task is easy, I score it a 1. If it's harder, it'll get a 2,3,5,8, etc. By adding up last week's total that I was able to complete, I can calculate my current "velocity" - this is the total amount of work I can accomplish in a given iteration and helps me schedule workload going forward. If you get into the practice of scheduling this way, it will scale well as your team grows.

If you want a platform that has all this built-in, Pivotal Tracker is a great bet. It's similar to Trello but built specifically for tracking software development and incorporates many of the principles above right out of the box.

Remember, even if you aren't coding your SaaS, you should still have a project management tool. This will be the source of truth for what's happening with your software and doesn't necessarily need to be limited to only software development tasks. Put everything in there and get used to using it every day to keep track of what needs to be done.

Use Your Calendar as a Guiding Light

As soon as you register your domain name, you need to have your calendar connected to every single device you access. Don't just access a Google Calendar through the browser. Instead, connect it to your desktop's calendar software and your mobile phone at a minimum.

Even before you have customers to pitch and demos to do, you'll have meetings you can't miss. These could be with potential partners, investors, software vendors, hosting providers, banks, etc. None of these are meetings you want to blow off. As you get deeper into your project, it will be difficult to keep up with everything without a solid reliance on a calendar app. So make sure you live and breathe by your calendar and set it to remind you of every meeting at least 10 minutes in advance (1 hour or more if you need to drive to get to it).

Tip: In addition to my work calendars, we actually keep a Google

Calendar for my family as well. I connect this everywhere my business calendar is connected and it makes it really easy to schedule meetings around personal commitments. My wife can add events to it to make sure I don't accidentally schedule a business meeting during something important. This is not required to build a SaaS product, obviously, but super handy!

Pen & Paper - it's a Classic!

If you're like me, organization is not your strong suit. I always feel so overwhelmed with the to-do lists that I need to complete and it can be hard for me to keep track of all my tasks on a computer or phone.

I started keeping a small notepad by my side to write down tasks that I need to complete. This simple organization tool has helped me feel more in control of what needs to get done, and it's much simpler than trying to manage everything on your computer or phone. Don't get me wrong - you still need project management software for tracking the work on your app, but for everything else, pen and paper is the way to go.

One thing you can do is create a list for each day with all the tasks you need to accomplish and you can also use this notepad to take notes in meetings so that they're always handy when you need them.

In fact, I've found it easier than using organization software because the tasks are all laid out in front of me on paper. It's much more straightforward: everything is right there! And if I need to write something down quickly, I just grab the pen and paper.

It's also nice to have a physical copy of your organization system, rather than an app. When you use the software on your laptop or phone, it can sometimes be difficult to locate certain tasks later because they're all stored in one place. Just by adding the date to the top of each page in your notepad, you can easily have a reference point and, by default, all of your pages are in chronological order.

I like to use a pen and paper because it's much easier to make notes from meetings. I don't have to worry about typing everything up afterward or having my hands tied just so I can type on the laptop in front of me (which is distracting - especially on video calls). When you're taking meeting minutes, tucking away your phone and grabbing a notepad can strike just the right balance.

Using pen and paper can be a good option for organization because it won't limit where or when you have access to your tasks. Anything you need to share digitally can be easily shared with a photo snapped on your phone and, even if the power goes out or a hard drive fails, you have full access to your notes.

Call me old school, but if it ain't broke, don't fix it.

Your Computer is Your Portal to the World

There's no denying that the world is becoming more and more connected every day via the internet. It's how we do our jobs, reach out to friends and family, stay informed on current events, and even keep up with social media. This also means that you can start your own business from just about anywhere in the world as long as you have a computer with an internet connection.

Your computer doesn't need to be the most modern piece of technology with the fastest speeds. Just about any laptop and any broadband connection will suffice. Your computer is your portal to the rest of the world: it's how you'll build and sell your products, attract customers, find investors, manage your finances – everything!

The only reason you would need to spend a lot on a computer is if you plan on doing a lot of photo or video editing. Even still, start with what you can and upgrade later. You don't want to use your computer's inadequacies as an excuse to not follow your dreams.

Laptops are highly portable and convenient for business people to carry around. They're also easier on your back so you can take them with you everywhere! The only downside is that laptops typically have smaller screens, so they might not be as good for photo editing or video work compared to a desktop computer – unless it's an expensive laptop designed specifically for the task.

Desktop computers, on the other hand, are better for photo and video editing as well and can help you get more done than on a laptop. They have larger screens that you can put up on a desk to work at all day and generally have more processing power for the money than laptops. However, the downside is that they are not as portable because they're big and heavy.

If your budget allows it, I'd recommend purchasing both laptop and desktop computers since each has its own advantages.

If you don't have two computers in the budget, you can always purchase a laptop computer and connect it to a monitor, keyboard, and mouse so you get the best of both worlds.

If you don't need a desktop, don't get one. This hybrid type of setup will set you up for just about any scenario.

Your Social Media Presence

If you have a social media account for your business, you are already on the right track. Social media is an important marketing tool and can help companies build awareness about their product or service. SaaS businesses in particular should use social media to find new customers who may be interested in what they offer. Social media gives you the ability to build an audience around your brand without having to pay for advertising.

If your SaaS is B2B, then LinkedIn is a must-have. On LinkedIn, you can find leads in your industry or those who are interested in the problems your product solves. With LinkedIn, you can target people based on their location and job title for higher conversion rates and more targeted leads. It's important not to just post content but also interact with others through posts, comments, shares, etc., so make sure you share quality information and have conversations rather than simply self-promotion by posting.

Most of your posts on your personal profile should have nothing to do with your product - make them purely value-based. When you want to say something about your business, share a post from your business page and write something about it in the post body.

Promotion through social networking channels may sound like a lot of work at first, but there are plenty of tools available that will help simplify the process as well as automate much of what needs to happen when posting updates (e.g., scheduling). Hootsuite, for instance, allows you to manage social media accounts from one central dashboard.

Social networks give you an opportunity for social interaction with your customers while getting the word out about your products and services, too.

Here are some tips for using social media effectively:

- Consider social media as a customer service channel.
- Be sure to have social media policies in place.
- Keep your posts relevant and on topic with what you're trying to accomplish.
- Use social listening tools to see what people are saying about your business, competitors, products, or services so that you can respond accordingly when appropriate (or even before the need arises). This will also help identify potential threats for future planning purposes.

Social media can provide you an organic, cost-free way to attract prospects, build community, and spread awareness for your business. Ensuring you have a presence on the major social channels could be the catalyst that sets you up for success.

Creating a Sustainable Process

Starting a business is tough. It requires discipline and an intense drive to succeed. You need to be ready for the long haul because success doesn't happen overnight. When things get hard, you have to work through them. If you want success, then you're going to need a lot of hard work and perseverance in your daily routine. To avoid burning out, make sure that you maintain a healthy balance between your work life and home life and don't push yourself too hard.

One way to keep from overdoing it is to stick to rigid systems. The systems you put in place need to be written in stone. Each day, you need to make sure you follow the same routine and work on your goals. You want success, so start now!

Once your systems are created, each night, before bedtime, review them for the next day. If they're not realistic or feasible, adjust accordingly until they fit into your lifestyle, otherwise, there's no point continuing down this path - you'll surely burn out and quit. You want a schedule you can maintain and execute consistently without impacting your personal life more than necessary - do everything you can to ensure your system is sustainable.

Here are some tips for staying motivated and refreshed:

- Take frequent breaks
- Drink plenty of water and eat healthily
- Exercise regularly
- Schedule in downtime every day so you can relax
- Get plenty of sleep each night (8-11 hours)

Work out your body as well as work on your mind by reading or listening to inspirational quotes or audiobooks. Take care of yourself, so you can reach success levels that will make you happy in the end! :)

You need to be disciplined about getting into bed at an appropriate time each night and waking up early enough every morning. Remember - success doesn't come overnight; it takes hard work and dedication over time. So give what you want from life all that you have.

Take care of yourself every day. Get plenty of rest. Stick to your process. This is how you create a sustainable and repeatable system for success.

Developing Great Ideas

Developing a great idea involves more than having an epiphany in the middle of the night. Great ideas can be created through a systematic and repeatable process. In short, identify a market, identify a niche within that market and then talk to people in that niche about their problems.

Identify Markets Close to You

In marketing, there is a term called product-market fit. It means that the marketing target demographic for your product matches up with the marketing target demographics of your business. This ensures that you are marketing to people who will buy your product and also helps you save money by not marketing to people who won't buy it. When deciding on a market to target for your SaaS product, start by identifying markets that you already know people in. Use those connections as springboards to connect with decision makers and get introductions into organizations that might want your product.

Everyone knows someone, right? Your personal connections may not be potential customers, but it's likely they know someone who would qualify as a prospect. The first step in determining a profitable market for your product is to identify it. So begin by identifying the markets you are already connected to when you're first getting started.

Let's look at an example of how this could work for you.

Susan is a 30-year old entrepreneur who just finished her MBA. She has been steadily working in marketing for the past five years but always knew that she wanted to start her own business. When Susan graduated, she decided to take some time off before starting on her own, and during this period, she met new people with different perspectives and ideas about entrepreneurship. After hearing these stories from friends of hers who had either started their own businesses or worked in startups, Susan was convinced that this was what she wanted to do next.

She first reached out to all of her friends - many of whom were connected with real estate - and asked them about potential markets where there would be demand for entrepreneurial talent like hers. She learned about the challenges they and their colleagues faced and, once Susan had a product to sell, her friends were able to connect her with local real estate agents in the areas they lived.

Over time, her business grew as did her network. Susan thought of the many meetings she had set up, and almost all of them were referrals from people in her network.

If Susan had created a product for startups or car dealerships, she might not have had the same level of success. By starting with an industry she was already tied into through her personal network, she was able to build a business based on relationships.

Understand Your Niche

The niche you choose to serve is vital to the success of your business. Finding a niche can be challenging, but it's worth it in the end because marketing to niche audiences has been shown time and time again as being successful.

What is a niche?

A niche is a subsection of your market that has specific needs. It could be as small as targeting people who work in the medical field who is left handed or it can encompass just about everyone with a pulse, like "healthy living". If you want to get really specific, you can choose a niche within a niche or "micro-niche". The more specific you get, the more you can speak directly to your customer, but the pool of customers available also shrinks. The goal is to find the sweet spot between too niche and too broad.

How do I find my niche?

Start by looking at what you know and asking yourself: What is unique about the problems my product solves? What niche in this market am I the best person to serve?

What are some examples of niche marketing for a business product or service?

- A virtual assistant company that focuses on hiring assistants who work exclusively from their homes and have experience with social media.
- An online teaching platform that trains teachers how to use tech-

nology in the classroom
- An online workout course for stay-at-home moms.
- Personal trainers for triathletes

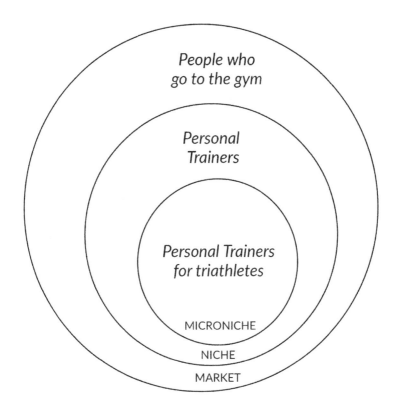

Choose a niche within your market or a micro-niche within a niche

In Susan's case, her niche was real estate agents who want custom

signs made. Her product, which lets real estate agents design and print their own signs fit in with the real estate market but gave her a smaller audience within that to target. By identifying independent agents who were also their own brokers, she was able to find clientele who were already searching for the product she was selling.

When you define your niche, you'll alienate the majority of your target market, but that's the whole point - you don't want to be speaking to everyone. You can reach niche customers with a more niche product or service that is "the best fit" for their needs.

This way, you'll establish stronger relationships with your audience, and build trust in your brand as they see themselves reflected on the page.

When you "niche down", you specialize. Being a specialist makes it easier to create effective messaging that drives action from your customers.

Analyze Market Size and Potential Reach

The smaller your niche is, the easier it will be to market to them. But this comes at a price since your overall audience size will be smaller.

Before locking in your niche, you need to analyze the market size to determine how many potential customers there are available to you. You'll also want to make sure this niche is something interesting to you since you will be spending a lot of your time immersed in it.

Some things to consider:

- Do you enjoy the niche market?
- Is there room for growth or is it saturated with competitors already?
- How much competition does your niche have at this time, and will that change soon (for instance, a pop culture trend)?
- How many potential customers are there in total?
- How much do those customers spend with your competitors?
- In a best-case scenario, how much could your business make per month in this market?

The factors above are only some of what you should keep in mind before choosing a niche. If you find your market will be too small in your niche, expand your criteria.

For instance, if your initial niche was going to be "WordPress plugin developers", maybe try expanding to "cms developers" or even "software developers" if it makes sense.

When you get so laser targeted that your audience shrinks, it will be harder to reach potential buyers simply because there are fewer of them. If you widen your net a little, you may find a larger market surrounding the initial niche that can also benefit from your product.

Who is in Your Niche and Your Network?

Once you've chosen a niche in a market you are connected to, the next step will be to identify which contacts you have that could provide insight into the problems faced by your prospective customers.

It might not be obvious at first, but as you go through your contact list and start thinking about the problems faced by customers in your niche, it becomes clear that many of them are connected to other people who will likely also need what you're selling. Maybe one of your contacts is an accountant so they know lots of accountants; another contact has been looking into hiring an engineer and knows several engineers they've recently interviewed; etc.

You can use this information to build up a network of highly interested prospects—people with real needs who come from networks that you are connected to, by referral. It's exciting to think how quickly these networks could grow once you get started and how warm the prospects will be when introduced to you by a mutual acquaintance.

Create a Pain Point Interview

Pain point interviews are an extremely powerful way to identify the pain points of your audience. When applied correctly, they can help you build a product that has widespread appeal and helps you generate more revenue. Once you've identified your initial network contacts, reach out and ask them some questions about their daily struggles at work.

Once you've identified a few common problems, ask them to rate these on a scale of one to ten and note if any other ideas come up in the conversation about those specific pain points. For example, maybe your contact mentions that she is often stuck at her desk because no matter what time of day it is or what kind of project she's working on, she'll be doing most tasks from an office setting for long periods of time. This may indicate that there could be some opportunity around helping people "work anywhere" which can also include times when they're traveling out-of-town and need access to important information.

These pain points will become the core of your product's value proposition.

When developing your pain point interview, you should have a goal in mind for each question you ask. For example, if you're trying to identify pain points related to marketing and want some solutions for this problem, ask questions that will help the interviewee remember a time when they experienced frustration in the marketing process at their company - maybe they implemented a solution that could be automated or improved upon.

Some examples of good pain point interview questions are:

- What frustrates you the most about your current marketing process?
- How do you find new prospects for your business?
- Which part of the sales pipeline is the hardest for you to manage and why?
- Which tools would be helpful in this area and which ones have been the most useful so far?
- What are some pain points or frustrations that come up when working with customers daily?
- If you could solve any one problem within your company, what would it be?

You can also ask open-ended questions like: "In general, how has your job affected your life outside of work?", ". What's the biggest surprise factor about starting at Company X?" etc.

The overarching goal of the interview process should be to identify opportunities. People don't pay for software with features, they pay for software that solves their problems. If you do the interviews over Zoom, you can record the conversation and refer back to it later. Make sure to get the other person's permission to record first, though.

After the interview, ask them to refer 3 colleagues they think would also participate in your interview. By getting a direct referral to these people, you not only will have more information from your pain point interviews, but you will also increase your network and may end up landing them as a customer down the road.

Reach out to these referral contacts and repeat the process until you have actionable ideas from their responses.

Turning Interviews Into Actionable Ideas

You might have noticed that some people in your niche share pain points with one another. That's a great start! Now it's time to dig deeper and find out what's behind those shared problems, so you can create a solution that tackles them head-on.

I once had a friend who was always complaining about how bad her feet hurt. When we dug deeper, she admitted that the shoes she wore all day long were pretty beat up and caused extra friction on top of blisters from before. She didn't realize until we talked about what could be going wrong with her feet that her shoes had been the problem the entire time.

The same logic applies to the answers you've received. The way someone phrases their pain is seldom in terms of the solution. If they knew the solution, they likely would have implemented it already.

You need to dig deeper to determine the root cause of the problems they experience. This is the only way you can know how to give them a solution that will actually work. When they tell you their feet hurt, you'll know you need to sell more comfortable shoes.

Take each of the pain points you'd like to focus on and make list with 3 columns. In the first column, put the pain point. In the second, put the cause. In the third, put a likely solution.

Pain Points	Causes	Solutions
My emails aren't getting delivered as expected.	Email list has bad addresses causing high bounce rate	Clean bad email addresses from list
My sales are lower than I think they should be	No good source of targeted leads to sell to	Get targeted, warm leads regularly

Make a list of pain points, causes, and solutions to brainstorm product ideas

The solutions column is where you should focus your ideas. Think of ways you could solve these problems with your software. At this point, you're getting closer to crafting a winning idea that will sell well.

Turning Insights Into a Winning Idea

Now you have fully evaluated the potential solutions to your target customer's problems, it's time to narrow it down to the best of the best for you to build as a business. Don't get too specific at this point. You want to leave your options open while specifically defining the value proposition of your idea. You can be more specific later when you've narrowed it down to the final idea.

At this point, you're trying to identify a high-level concept rather than specific features you'll build into your product. For instance, instead of deciding to build an online real estate agent directory, you might say "My business will help independent realtors promote themselves for less".

Once you have this "mission statement" created for your product, make a shortlist of things that could accomplish your objective. In this case, you might choose some things like "Realtor advertising network", "Helping Realtors get yard signs" or "A realtor directory that gives realtors a web presence". These more targeted descriptions can help you shape the idea further.

Naming Your Idea

Once you have settled on a concept, start brainstorming names. Make a list of at least 20 names that you like for your idea. Get creative here and try to come up with names that are short (less than 10 characters), catchy, and easy to remember. Once you have your list complete, start crossing them off.

Here you can be super picky - if a name just sounds weird or irks you for some odd reason, just cross it off. Pay close attention to your first impressions of these names as you go through them, this will be your last opportunity to view them with new eyes.

As you narrow it down, you may want to get feedback from family, friends, or coworkers to help you choose the best of what you have. Once you get the name locked down, it will be time to buy a domain name and validate your idea as a whole.

Tip: Pull up GoDaddy as you are choosing names and search for the .com version of your names. Make a note next to each one where the .com address is available and give these preference when making the final call.

Choosing a Great Domain Name

The domain name is the first impression your visitors will get when they visit your website. A good domain name can set a positive tone for the rest of their experience, while a bad one might cause them to leave in frustration before even looking at what you have to offer. That is why it's so important that you purchase a high-quality domain and build a brand around it. Since you've spent so much time choosing the perfect name, you want to make sure you get a domain to match, but that can be harder than you think.

There are currently 4.6 billion people on earth with access to the internet. That's your competition for the domain name you want. As more people come online every day and new websites are created, domain names become more and more scarce. This means you either have to be really lucky, really creative or have a bunch of cash to buy the domain you want from someone else.

Being creative is my method of choice. At this point, getting stuck on a domain name that will cost you $20k isn't worth it. Instead, keep coming up with names or permutations of your domain until you can find one available. This is how you snag your domain for as low as $0.99 and have it match your brand. But the first thing you need to do is pick a domain registrar to register your domain with.

Choosing a Domain Registrar

A domain registrar is a company that you pay to register your domain and allow you to operate your website using it. While the domain registrar may offer website hosting, they don't necessarily need to. You can just register your domain with them and use their DNS services to point the domain at your hosting provider of choice.

Choosing the right domain name registrar can be a difficult and confusing process. There are dozens of companies out there that offer similar services, but it's important to find one that is reputable, has competitive pricing, and offers everything you need to get your website up and running fast.

You should pay attention to things like downtime notifications, ease of use, and accessibility across all platforms including mobile apps if possible, as well as security features for both domains and privacy protection. Some companies offer free WHOIS privacy protection on their plans which means that they will hide your personal information from public access - which is nice if your site picks up traction. The key is finding the right combination of these features that fit within your budget.

A couple of reputable domains registrars are:

* GoDaddy - Offers .COM domains at a reasonable price with some of the most flexible plans to choose from, including free WHOIS privacy protection on all their registration packages for any new customers who sign up or renew.

* NameCheap - Low prices make this company great for beginners and

it covers 100% of ICANN's registration fees. It also offers several useful tools like domain parking, private domains, and the ability to transfer your .COM/.NET/.ORG/.BIZ/cc TLD to NameCheap easily.

Some registrars may also provide additional benefits, such as discounts on hosting or SSL certificates. Be sure to do your research so you know what all the options are for domain registration and choose wisely based on your needs.

Whatever registrar you choose, make sure you enable auto-renew on your domain name. If your domain expires, the registrar could lock it up for months and you might not be able to get it back before someone else snags it.

Do your research, choose wisely and make sure to keep auto-renew turned on for all your domains!

Choosing the Right TLD

Choosing a TLD (top-level domain) for your website can be confusing. There are many different options, and some of the most popular include .com, .org, and .net. The best option is to use the domain name that everyone recognizes: .com. This will help you get more traffic from people who know how to find your site on search engines like Google or Yahoo!

It may be tempting to get your domain as a .net or .co, but it will confuse your customers and they will have trouble visiting your website. The exceptions to this would be companies utilizing artificial intelligence having the .ai TLD or for companies only operating in one country to use a country-specific TLD like .co.uk.

Domain Name Variations

If the domain name you want isn't available in .com, try some variations. For instance, if your app was called "Microphone" and the domain microphone.com isn't available, you could add a prefix to the domain like "usemicrophone.com". Be creative and try to go for a .com address that someone could spell if they heard it on the radio.

The use of prefixes and suffixes is pretty widespread these days so don't be surprised to find that even some odd variations of your product name may be taken. Common prefixes and suffixes you might use are "use-" ,"try-", "get-", "-app", "-pro", etc. You can also add suffixes like "-ify", "-osity" to your product name - the possibilities are endless. Don't feel constrained by "real words" and, instead, try to snag something catchy and makes sense alongside your value proposition.

Making a List of Available Domains

As you're searching for domain names, you'll find names you like that are available. Don't buy them yet. Put them all on a list - get around 20-30 if you can. Share this list with family members and friends to see which ones stick out most in their minds. If there's a common trend among their responses then congratulations-you have found your perfect domain name!

Tip: When you're choosing your domain name, try to find one that is memorable. This will allow people who hear it from a friend to easily remember it and come back later!

Expired Domain Lists

Expired domain lists can be a treasure trove of great domains. If you haven't settled on a name, searching expired lists might turn up something great or inspire you to come up with something new.

When purchasing an expired domain, you want to make sure you know a little bit about its history. You don't want a domain that has previously been associate with spam or faked page rank, otherwise, it may already be on deliverability blacklists or have other issues that you wouldn't encounter with a new domain.

On the flip side, expired domains can come with a history that helps you as well. For instance, if the domain had previously belonged to an active site that published new content regularly and had a great reputation, you'd be inheriting that as well.

Knowing the full history of an expired domain can help you avoid pitfalls associated with them and open you up to new ideas and great deals.

Validating Your Idea

The product validation process is all about figuring out what people want and need. Validating your product idea will save you a ton of time, money, and headaches in the long run because it gives you an answer to the question: "Is this product something people actually want?" When developing a product, it's crucial that you validate before wasting any more time or resources on something that has no demand.

To validate that your idea is sound, you'll want to test the market. Luckily, you already have some contacts in your niche that are willing to provide feedback. Now you just need a branded product to present to them to gauge their interest and a high-converting landing page for them to interact with, giving you both data on the validity of your idea, but also contact information for potential customers who are already interested in your product.

Creating Your Brand

Your brand is important because it conveys so much about your business to your customers and prospects. Ultimately, your brand will matter to the future buyer of your business as well. The more excited you can make them, the easier it will be to sell.

Your brand defines how people think about your business and how describe you to others. When creating your brand, it's important to kee this in mind, making sure you have something you are genuinely proud to share with the world and something worth talking about.

Your brand is made up of your purpose, your voice, and your identity. These elements can be broken down further to:

- **Logo (Identity)**: Your logo is a snapshot of your brand that can be quickly absorbed. It should represent your company culture through color, fonts, and basic imagery
- **Color Palette (Identity)**: Colors interact with customers on a sub-conscious level and convey the general mood that your brand portrays (excited, relaxed, cool, etc).
- **Tagline (Voice)**: Your tagline is a single phrase that says what your company is all about
- **Tone of Voice (Voice)**: This is the tone of voice (happy, casual, formal, laid back, etc) your brand "speaks" in. All of your copy should be in this tone.
- **Fonts (Identity)**: Using the same fonts throughout all of your marketing materials will make it easy for people to recognize your brand and become familiar with it
- **Images (Voice)**: The images you use may show your ideal customers, how to use your product, common problems. They may be illustrations or photographs.
- **Positioning (Purpose)**: This is your niche and how you serve your target market. Your niche should be conveyed through your brand.

If you aren't skilled at creating graphics for your logo, colors, fonts, and imagery, you can find someone on Fiverr or use a service like Design Pickle to help.

ndation for your brand is the first step to validating
everything else stems from your brand and your
Take the principles, language, imagery, and vibe
...oped so far into every other step of the process going
forward.

Know Your Personas

Your brand should portray itself to your target audience as though it is
their best friend and has solutions to all their problems. This means you
need to know them inside and out.

One way to come up with your initial brand positioning is to create
a fictional avatar of your ideal customer. Give them a name and a
backstory. Write down a story involving them as the main character and
cover these points:

- Where they work (i.e. A corporate office)
- How long they've been there (i.e. Less than 1 year)
- Where they struggle (i.e. Keeping track of customer support emails)
- What they want out of life (i.e. To impress their new boss)

When you know what your customer wants, it's much easier to speak
to them. If you target different customer personas then go through
this exercise a few more times. Each persona should be targeted with a
unique landing page, speaking just to them.

Creating a Landing Page

There are a lot of ways you can validate your product idea, but creating a landing page is one of the best. A landing page allows people to see what they'll be getting into if they purchase your product - without having to spend any money at all. It also will allow you to collect email addresses from people who are excited about your product launch and ready to buy when the product is live.

A landing page is a simple, one-page website that has nothing on it but your product. Usually, you'll have something like "Get Started" or "Try It Now" to get people interested in their purchase and then some form of payment at the end (sometimes even just a link). The goal of the landing page will be to collect email addresses for people who would be interested in the product.

Think about it - if you can't get people to give you their email address for the promise of something that could solve their problem, then why would you expect them to pay you? The best ideas collect email addresses quickly and easily from their landing pages while the ideas you should avoid will have landing pages with empty mailing lists, gathering dust.

It's not just collecting email addresses, though. Landing pages are a great way to test how much people want your product and also get feedback about what they think of the general idea (which you may or may not have thought was already awesome). It's important to validate that this is an effective solution for them.

When building your page, make sure the focus is completely on inform-ing the user of what your product will be and collecting their contact information. No navigation, no banner ads - nothing that will distract from the task at hand.

You'll want all the copy to be very benefit-driven vs feature-driven which is great at this stage since you still don't have a concrete product roadmap. Offering a load of benefits with a promise to notify them when the product is ready is generally enough to get most people over the line if the idea is good.

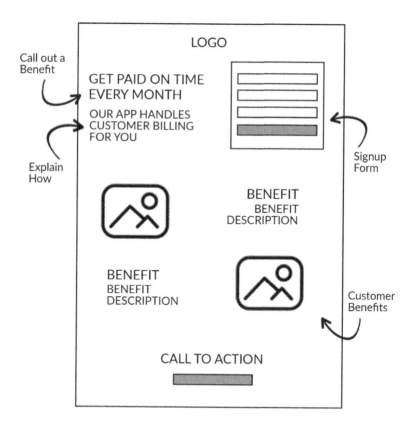

Keep your landing page focused on getting your visitor to take action

Ensure you also only have a single call to action. Having multiple calls to action will confuse your visitors and lower the conversion rate. There are some places where having multiple calls to action can be ok - in the footer of a website, for instance - but on a landing page, the ask of the visitor should be crystal clear and limited to one thing - collecting their contact info.

It should go without saying that you need to test this page on as many devices as possible. Most of your visitors will probably be using mobile devices so you want to make sure you use responsive design so it looks and functions great on desktops, laptops, tablets, and smartphones.

Share your landing page with the contacts you've already interviewed and ask them for their feedback. Most people, when discussing how someone else can solve their problems, will gladly participate.

Promoting on Social Media

Since you have your landing page up and running, another great place to promote it is social media. You can post to your profile, in relevant groups, etc to gauge the response to your idea from strangers.

Make sure you aren't spamming groups though. No one really needs to see the link to your landing page more than once to decide if they are interested. If your idea is good, people will click on your post and sign up on the landing page - no doubt about it. If no one is engaging with your posts, or signing up on your landing page, it's a decent indication that you need to work on improving your product idea and solution.

You can also reach out to prominent figures in your niche via LinkedIn.

You may be surprised at how willing people are to provide you feedback on your idea. Don't expect everyone to respond, but send a message like "Hey! I'm working on an idea that I think could solve [the problem it solves]. Would you mind taking just a moment and providing feedback on what I'm working on?" works more times than it doesn't.

Measuring Engagement

It may seem like landing pages are just landing pages. However, they play a HUGE role in your marketing and sales process and should not be overlooked. Landing page engagement can measure what your visitors care about most and knowing your conversion rate (the percentage of people who take action on your landing page) can help you determine overall interest in your offering.

When measuring landing page engagement, make sure you know the three metrics below:

Total Traffic Volume – total number of landing page visitors

Interaction Rate – total interactions divided by the landing page visitor volume

Conversion Rate – landing page conversion rate is calculated as the percentage of a landing page's unique visitors who have taken specific action on that particular landing page (e.g. provided an email)

You can measure your total traffic volume by installing Google Analytics on your landing page. You can also set up javascript events in Google Analytics to track things like button clicks or video views.

To measure your conversion rate, you'll want to take the total number of email addresses you've collected in a given timeframe and divide it by the total traffic from Google Analytics in the same timeframe.

Here is a formula to calculate the conversion rate:

Conversion Rate (%) = (Total Emails / Total Traffic) x 100

For example, if you have a total of 500 landing page visitors and 20 email addresses that were collected during the time period, your conversion rate will be 4%.

Having a high conversion rate (> 30%) along with high traffic volume is a great indicator of good product-market fit and means that your idea will likely resonate well with your niche audience.

Generating Social Engagement

Now that you have a validated idea and a killer domain name, you'll want to start building a community around your niche. To do this for free (ie. without spending money on ads), turn to social media.

For B2B (business to business) SaaS, LinkedIn is the place to be. For B2C (business to consumer) SaaS, any number of social networks will work - really whatever is trending the most today.

Regardless of the platform you choose, the same basic principles apply. Your goal is to assert yourself as an authority in your niche and provide value to people who are connected with you. As you build connections, you'll build trust. Your network will become your sounding board for new ideas and a way to gain customers when you are ready to launch.

I'll assume you're building a B2B SaaS for this section and focus primarily on LinkedIn.

Polishing Up Your Profile

LinkedIn is a powerful social network for professionals. Unfortunately, many people don't take the time to set up their profiles in a way that will help them generate more leads and connections with potential clients. You need to set up your LinkedIn profile to maximize its effectiveness.

Here are some things to check on your profile:

Headshot: A headshot that best represents who you are as a person or company - this needs to be at least 400px by 400px in size, but it can also be larger than this for better quality.

Tip: Bright-colored backgrounds attract the most attention when people are scrolling through their timelines.

Experience Section: This is the main section of your profile where you should list all your experience. Make sure to include the CEO of your new venture as the most recent position!

Contact Information: Contact information for people wanting more information from you. Provide your website address, email address, and phone number. If you don't want to share your phone number, get a Google Voice number and use that.

Projects: Include your projects (including your new business when it's ready) including links to the work you have done, or skills you possess. You can also include testimonials from customers at this point as well if you have them.

Summary Headline: This should summarize what it is about yourself

49

that potential followers would find most valuable so they know whether to connect with you. Something like "I help businesses do XYZ..." or "Founder of XYZ Product"

Profile Description: A short paragraph about you and your business. This is the most viewed portion of your profile. Make sure it conveys who you are and what you do in an easy-to-consume manner.

When you post on LinkedIn, people will check out your profile to see what you're about. This is your chance to make a great first impression, provide value, and (hopefully) gain a follower. The better your profile looks, the more likely someone is to follow you. Make sure you are honest and transparent, though. Lying on your profile won't get you anywhere - people will find out and then won't want to work with you anymore.

Likes and Comments

One of the best ways to grow your audience on LinkedIn is by liking and commenting on other people's posts. This not only helps them but also increases the chance that they will follow you back or click on one of your links.

The LinkedIn newsfeed is curated based on algorithms that choose which posts someone should see. It works by checking a person's engagement with posts and their connections to other people. This means that if you like and comment on someone else's post, it is not only more likely they will see your comment but also the next time they login it will appear at the top of their feed because of this engagement.

Commenting on another LinkedIn user's post will have the effect of showing up on their newsfeed and also the posts of people to whom they are connected.

To put this in perspective, if a person has 100 connections each with 50 followers, that comment will reach out to 5000 potential users just by commenting one time! This doesn't mean they will all see it, but if the engagement is good, they definitely could.

Additionally, interacting with real people in a genuine, non-transactional way will help you build relationships with people in your niche. Relationships are the foundation of how business deals get done and partnerships are made. If you want to scale your business in the future, start building your network right now.

Creating Valuable Content In Your Niche

You won't gain much of a following if you don't post to LinkedIn. The good news is you don't have to be creative to do it. You just need the proper system in place. In short, write about your niche every day. Be consistent in the topics you cover. Offer actionable advice that people can follow.

Writing about the same topic every day asserts your authority on the topic and attracts people interested in that topic to you. If you write about too many different things, you won't be "known" for anything. Instead, stick with the niche your SaaS product is in.

The posts that get the best responses are posts that offer actionable advice. Actionable advice is advice people can implement right now. It's not just a list of tips or links to other posts on the topic (though those are helpful too).

Actionable advice would be things that solve problems in your niche. Remember all those answers to your pain point interviews? Use them for content ideas! Pick a pain point (any pain point from your interviews) and post about how to solve the problem. The solution may not have anything to do with your product and that's ok. What you're doing is providing value so that others will see you as someone who can solve their problems.

Posting once a day (during the workweek at least) will grow your following gradually over time. This is why it's so important to start now before you even have a product to sell. When your product is ready to launch, you want an engaged audience to sell it to.

Don't Buy Social Engagement

Buying followers on social media may make your brand appear to have reach, but those followers can hurt you. In addition to real people finding out that your followers are fake and losing trust in you, buying followers will actually make your posts perform worse.

Social networks decide what posts to show people based on internal algorithms that take into account many variables to determine which content is the most relevant. One of the major factors at play is a post's traction. A post's traction can be determined by looking at the number of engagements over the first few hours the post is online.

When a social network is looking at the traction of a post, they will compare the engagement with the expected engagement based on the size of the author's network. Do you see where this is going? If your network is filled with bots who follow you, they won't be engaging with your content and leaving valuable comments. Instead, it will appear to the algorithm that your post was really unpopular with your audience. This can actually spread to your account over time, having your account flagged as not posting valuable content – all because you wanted a large follower count on your page. This can essentially render all your efforts on social media useless.

Instead of buying followers, create real relationships with people. Grow your following organically by creating valuable content and sharing it. The more you put into it, the more you'll get out of it.

Perfecting Your Pricing

When it comes to SaaS pricing, there are several different models that you can choose from. In this section, we will discuss the various types and their pros and cons. The pricing model you choose will have a great impact on your future revenue, so it's good to give some thought now to where you want your business to go in the future to choose the best fit.

Types of SaaS Pricing Models

The most prevalent model in SaaS is a plan-based subscription model. In this scenario, you offer several different plans, each with varying features or resources, that your customers can choose from. This allows you to cater your service specifically to their needs. The benefit of this model is that customers place themselves on their preferred plan and generally end up paying for resources they don't use. This can mean more revenue for you, but it also means the customers are overpaying sometimes if you are monetizing usage.

Another common way to bill your customers is through metered subscriptions. With metered subscriptions, the customer pays monthly and the amount changes from month to month based on their usage of your software. This is a great model if you are monetizing a lot of transactional events like sending SMS messages. If your offering is primarily feature-based, then metered subscriptions may not be the right option for you.

One strategy that the plan-based model is great for is selling annual subscriptions. Since the plan costs the same every month, you can offer your customers a discount if they pay for the entire year in advance. This gives you more cash to put into acquiring new customers sooner.

It's important to think about pricing in the very early stages of your company. The type of pricing model you choose will help you determine how to build your application and how to position your product in the market.

Freemium Pricing

Freemium pricing in SaaS is a double-edged sword.

Once upon a time, there was a way of selling software where you'd charge money and provide the product. Nowadays it's more common to offer your service for free but implemented with an option to buy into the premium version. This is called freemium pricing and has been one of the most successful business models in recent years.

When executed properly, freemium plans are excellent because their goal is not immediate profit but rather a long-term gain through customer satisfaction by providing access to basic features for free while offering advanced or "premium" features only via subscription plans that cost money.

The hope here is that customers will eventually be persuaded to convert and purchase a subscription plan. The conversion rate for freemium pricing is actually very high, nearly 30% of all users who see the free version convert to paying customers on average.

But this model also has its drawbacks:

Freemium prices provide limited control over product usage because it's so easy for people to sign up and use your service without ever buying anything at all. This can lead to an increased cost in terms of hosting resources or bandwidth as well as customer support costs since many more people than anticipated may start using your service on a given day.

One strategy you could employ here would be limiting user access by setting time limits (i.e., two hours per month) or imposing quotas (i.e., only one gigabyte of data).

Overall, we can see why freemium pricing has been so successful: it's an excellent way to build customer loyalty by providing basic features at no cost while still generating some income through advanced features.

At the same time though, there are some drawbacks such as increased hosting/bandwidth expenses and having less control over usage patterns due to limited access (time limits or quotas) being imposed on users who aren't paying customers yet. As with any strategy - you need to weigh the pros and cons to make the best decision.

Identifying Your Competition

I am sure you have heard the phrase "price equals value" before. It is true! If your pricing is set too high, then your product will be competing with premium products in its market space. On the other hand, if it is priced too low, then it becomes a commodity and competes with other companies who offer similar features at lower prices. Let's discuss how to use competitive analysis to help optimize your SaaS product's pricing strategy.

An easy way to see if your pricing is set at the right level is the compare its pricing and features to other products in the market. Find the lowest-priced product and the highest-priced products. You'll find that many of the products with the same functionality are serving different market segments at different price points. Now you need to figure out where your business falls in comparison to the existing players.

Make a list of who you think your competitors are. Write down their prices, trial lengths and any major features that you think are an important part of the customer's buying decision.

For example, if, in your market, the customer's decision is largely dependent on whether they like a product's interface or not then that should be one of your top features in this analysis.

This list will give you an idea of what to focus on when you write about these competitors because there are certain aspects and features which might matter more than others for them (rather than having all customers make their buying decisions based solely on price).

For example, some companies may care most about how long it takes to get started with a competitor while other firms prioritize security – so knowing what matters to each company is crucial information for understanding how they'll react to your pricing.

Now, decide where you want your business to fall on that list. You could be the cheapest, but people will perceive you as cheap. You could be the most expensive and people may perceive you as more valuable, but as a new business, can you compete against the whales in your market who likely have millions in the bank? You might be able to pull it off with the right feature set, but, in the spirit of repeatable results, I'd suggest you find somewhere in the middle you can shine.

As an example, pricing your plans comparable to the mid to lower range in your market, but offering features that compete with the high end can land you in a sweet spot since your cost to value ratio will be off the charts. This makes your product an easy sell against mid-range competitors.

Once you have figured out where you fall, make a list of all the competitors in your price range. These are the companies you need to beat. There may be 100 other businesses in the market at higher or lower price points, but your customers likely won't go to them out of cost or quality concerns alone – especially if you can deliver a robust feature set at a fair price.

Double Your Prices

Say what?

Once you've got some customers (at least 100-200) on board and feel like you've achieved product-market fit, double your prices. It feels crazy, but, as long as you grandfather existing customers into their original price, trust me - no one will notice and your new acquisition revenue will double overnight. If someone does complain that they were expecting the previous price, just set them up on the original pricing and they will be happy.

I've done this on almost every platform I've worked on and have only had a handful of people reach out about it. Most people don't remember the exact dollar amount for a product, but, instead, they think of an estimated amount vs the product's value.

If your product was $120/mo, people might remember it as "around $100 or so, but more than $100, but totally worth it cause you get like $500 in value". Doubling to $240, they might notice it's more than they remember, but the value is still there and they won't split hairs with you.

If you do encounter any friction, remember you can always lower your prices and people will be happy, so keep that as a backup. It's better to have room to negotiate than to already be as low as you can go.

Flexible Pricing

It's important to remember that you won't be able to anticipate the needs of every customer in advance. You might have large companies reach out to you who need more than your plans support. This is why you should make sure to build in a flexible pricing model that can be engaged on a per-customer basis.

Many SaaS platforms call this "Enterprise Pricing". Essentially, it allows you to make custom deals with each customer on an individual basis. This can definitely be used to land a whale of a customer by giving them a volume discount, but it can also be used to close sales with price-sensitive customers at any level.

Remember, it's better to acquire a customer at a slightly lower rate, than for them to bounce over to your competitors. In SaaS, the margins are generally very high, so you should have plenty of wiggle room to negotiate your price - just make sure your software can keep up with your sales efforts.

Offering Free Trials

Many SaaS apps implement a free trial period. This gives customers the ability to sign up and try the product for a specified time without paying. At the end of the trial, they can either pay to continue using the product or they can cancel their account if they don't feel it was right for them.

Most trials are either 7, 14, or 30 days. Some apps will go as long as 90 days. So how do you decide how long the trial should be? I'd start by looking at how long it takes to get value from your app. For instance, if your app lets business owners send monthly reminders to their customers, then a 7-day trial won't afford them enough time for the reminders to even be sent out. However, if your app adds a lead collection form to a customer's website, then they should be able to see it working pretty quickly.

The main idea is to not have the customer's trial end before they receive value. In fact, many companies, at the end of the trial, allow customers to extend it for another week or two. This can not only keep them around until they see the value in your product, but it can also help your team identify new customers that could use help in using the app to its greatest potential.

If your app has a free plan, you may not want to include a trial. After all, they can use the free plan to try the app out, right? That may work for some apps, but I've found that having a trial on a paid plan will get more people onto your paid plans – especially if you have a free plan.

Regardless of how you decide to run your free trials, remember that the main goal of a trial is to show value and retain customers. Don't get hung up on the fact that they aren't paying you for the app during this time. They may not be spending money, but they are *spending time on your app* and that's the best thing you can get a potential customer to do.

Payment Processing

Choosing a payment provider for your SaaS can be challenging. Numerous companies provide payment services, and each one has its own transaction fees, chargeback fees, and costs to implement. If you have a marketplace component in your SaaS, then you will also want to make sure you are familiar with the liability that is on your customer, yourself, and the payment provider.

What's the Cost to Implement?

The first thing to consider is the cost to implement. Many payment providers that have been around for a long time have antiquated APIs and documentation making them more difficult for developers to work with. On the other hand, they also generally have the most publicly available code libraries and CMS plugins. Your decision on the cost to implement should be based on your own developer resources.

Transaction Fees

Next, you need to think about transaction fees and chargeback fees. Transaction costs depend a lot on the volume of transactions that will go through your SaaS as well as if they are credit or debit payments. Some providers have different rates for what is called "card-present" transactions which means deals were made in person with physical cards versus "card-not-present" meaning online purchases from merchants without an actual card present at any point during the purchase process. This distinction can also affect how much work it takes for you to set up integrations with each provider when both types exist within their API's architecture and documentation sets.

Since you'll be transacting primarily online, "card-present" fees will likely not apply to you. Instead, you may look at companies that aggregate the credit card fees. This is how businesses like Stripe and PayPal arrive at their rates. They essentially average out all the fees across the major card providers (MasterCard, Visa, Amex, etc) and charge a flat rate of 2.9% + $0.30 per transaction. Even though Amex may charge a higher rate, the number of MasterCard and Visa transactions is much higher on their platforms, so they actually end up making more from fees than if they charged more in line with their costs.

While you may be thinking "Well I'd just go with the company with the lowest fees", that cost to implement comes into play. Companies like Stripe, PayPal, Braintree, and Authorize.Net all provide a plethora of docs, libraries, and resources. Finding developers that can work within their systems is fairly easy due to their prominence in the market.

Stripe and PayPal both offer low-code options to integrate with them and, although the costs may be more than a traditional merchant account, you can be up and running in a matter of hours.

High-Risk Merchant Accounts

If you are selling anything in an industry that's considered "high-risk" (ie. cannabis, guns, gambling, adult content, etc). Then the processors everyone else is using likely won't work for you. Stripe and PayPal both keep a long list of prohibited businesses that they refuse to work with.

In this case, you should look at getting a high-risk merchant account. You can interface with most of these accounts via Authorize.Net. While the cost to implement may be similar to Stripe and PayPal, the fees will not be. High-risk merchant accounts can have fees that are as low as two or three percent or as high as twelve or thirteen percent.

Disputed Transactions (Chargebacks)

You should also make sure to read the terms and agreements for each provider you are considering to find out what your liability is in various situations. Generally, when a transaction is disputed, you will have to repay the funds immediately and will also assume an extra chargeback fee of $15-50, depending on the provider.

Chargebacks can be a huge pain so you want to avoid them at all costs. One major reason that SaaS companies experience chargebacks is automatically billing a customer at the end of their trial. Many may forget they agreed to pay and, without a signature, it will be hard to prove they agreed to the customer's bank - leaving you out the revenue and the chargeback fee. This can be avoided by locking their account at the end of the trial and asking them to input their credit card info then instead of during signup.

Another reason you may see chargebacks is if you implement annual billing. While this can be a great way to get more revenue upfront, if you don't have clear reminders leading up to the renewal date, you could have some surprised customers when they get hit with an entire year's charges out of the blue.

Make sure you communicate well with your customers and they understand when and how much they will be billed and you shouldn't have to sweat too much about getting hit with chargebacks and additional fees.

PCI Compliance & Security

Once you have credit card processing secured, you'll also need to think about your security. To accept payments online, your checkout process needs to be PCI Compliant. PCI Compliance is a set of security standards enforced by the card associations.

If you are worried about PCI Compliance, a good solution is to get an external payment gateway that will integrate into your website so that it becomes PCI Compliant for you like Stripe or PayPal.

You'll also want to make sure you have an SSL certificate installed on your website once you have that up and running. In addition to helping with security, an SSL will also give you a boost in the search engine results pages as well. You can either purchase an SSL through your hosting provider or generate one for free with LetsEncrypt's free SSL service.

Tokenizing Credit Card Numbers

Tokenization is a process that replaces sensitive data with substitute information or "tokens." Tokenization can be used to protect cardholder data, as well as other types of personal data. When you use tokenization correctly, the original payment account number and expiration date are not stored anywhere on your servers. Instead, they're replaced by one-time tokens created from public/private encryption keys - which means hackers cannot get them since there's no way for unauthorized parties to know what the real value should have been.

Tokenization is an effective way to protect your customers from having their personal data stolen and used for fraudulent purchases or other illegal activities. It also protects your company by reducing fraud levels which means more revenue! The best part about tokenization is that you can still charge your customers and accept payments from them without storing sensitive information on your servers. When a customer makes a purchase, the credit card number would be replaced with a random set of numbers known as tokens. The system does not store any personal data which means it cannot be stolen or used for fraudulent purchases or other illegal activities.

All major payment gateways today support tokenization out of the box. Payment gateways that do not support tokenization shouldn't be in the running for your app at all. Save yourself the headache and only work with companies who implement tokenization and sleep better at night knowing your customers' sensitive data is safe and secure.

Understanding the Customer Journey

The customer journey is a term used to describe the process that customers undergo when they interact with your business. Understanding this concept will help you build better relationships with potential and existing customers, which in turn helps you generate more sales for your business.

It's important to understand the customer journey before you begin building your product so you can put yourself in the shoes of your future users. You'll want to know what stage in the customer journey your product is going to be most helpful for, which will help you develop a marketing strategy.

Your first step would be understanding where customers are during each phase of their journey with your business and how they're feeling at that point. For example, if someone is looking through reviews online before making a purchase decision about your company's product or service then they could easily feel overwhelmed as there might be hundreds of reviews for different products on multiple sites - so it can seem difficult to find the best one.

You should also know all the points along their path from consideration (e.g., browsing social media) all the way up until conversion - when they buy something from you-that could influence their decision to purchase.

The customer journey can be visualized by a funnel shape. When you visualize the "sales funnel", it can help you figure out the best approach to take with each prospect based on where they are in their buying process.

What's a Marketing & Sales Funnel?

A typical marketing funnel starts with a large number of potential customers at the top and narrows down to just those who are most likely to buy from you, as they move through your sales process. The wider the top section of the funnel is, the more people will enter it; but if you can narrow the top section, you'll be able to make more sales.

Your marketing funnel represents a long-term process that moves people from awareness of your company or product through different stages of consideration until they become customers and then repeat purchasers over time. The key goal is to attract new prospects into the pipeline to maintain a steady flow of new customers.

The top of the funnel is where you find people who are just beginning to search for a product like yours. The middle of the funnel refers to those prospects that have started looking into what your company offers and has either purchased something or expressed intent in buying from your business. At the bottom, we have customers who make a purchase, followed by those who buy regularly from your company and may even be considered brand ambassadors—people who spread awareness about your products through word-of-mouth marketing.

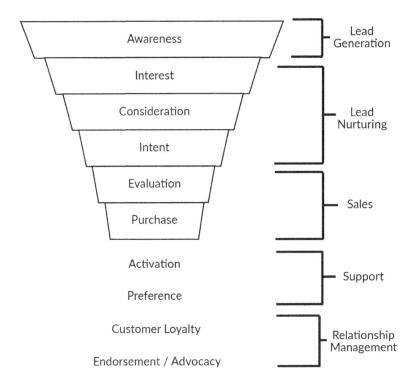

Understanding the customer journey is vital to successful sales

Each level represents different characteristics related to customer behavior as they move down the funnel:

· **Awareness** – The awareness step of the funnel is when you're just introducing your product or service to the marketplace. You'll want to spend your time trying to establish trust and credibility.

- **Interest** - The next step is the interest phase, where customers are interested in solving their problem and they are aware of your product.
- **Consideration** - In the consideration phase, the customer is aware of your product, interested in solving their problem, and is considering using your product to do it. They are likely considering your competitors as well.
- **Intent** - In the intent phase, the customer is looking to buy something as soon as possible. This is when you'll want to really work hard on perfecting the customer's experience and make sure they're getting everything that they need all in one place: from pricing, availability, or delivery information, right down to any additional add-ons that might be appropriate for their purchase.
- **Evaluation** - It's not until the evaluation stage that a customer will think about buying your product or service specifically. Here, you're trying to make sure they feel confident and reassured in their choice by providing them with as much information as possible so it is easy for them to buy from you.
- **Purchase** - The final phase of the funnel is purchase! At this point, the customer commits to doing business with you, and money is exchanged.

After the funnel, you have the continuation of the customer journey where customer support and relationship management come into play.

- **Activation** - Activating the customer entails getting them to be excited to be users of your platform. Activated customers have their accounts set up and are avid users of your product.
- **Preference** - When customers become "preferred," they've indicated that your product is their favorite and they're only interested in receiving information about you or offers from you.

- **Loyalty** - Loyal customers are those who have shown a long-term interest in your product. They're dependable and you can count on them to continue using it or purchasing from you.
- **Advocacy** - In the final stage of the customer journey, advocacy is when customers are actively promoting you to their friends and family.

It's important to understand where each of your customers is in their journey so you can identify with them, solve their specific needs, and communicate with them more effectively. For instance, people visiting your homepage could be at any stage of the funnel, but people checking out your pricing page are likely in the consideration stage. Similarly, someone in the midst of their free trial would be in the evaluation stage while someone who has been a customer for 6 months might be an advocate for you.

Establishing Trust

Building relationships is the most important part of any sales process because it's all about building trust—trust between you and your customer, plus trust for their business partners (e.g., vendors) where applicable.

Establishing trust is crucial to any sale. The creation of an emotional bond begins when a salesperson first interacts with a prospect or when a prospect visits your website and continues through every subsequent interaction.

Steps for Building Trust:

- **Explain your company's mission statement:** share who you are, what you do, how long you've been in business, where your head-quarters are located; these details can go a long way toward building trust.
- **Demonstrate knowledge about their industry:** research competi-tors, know the ins and outs of particular industries' unique termi-nology so that customers feel like they're talking to someone on their level—this demonstrates empathy as well as knowing how difficult it is to run a small business (or a large one!)
- **Actively listen:** when you're on a call, be an active listener. This means not just letting the customer do all the talking (though that's important) but actually listening to what they are saying and responding with empathy.

Make plans with the customer journey in mind. Establish trust with your customers by truly understanding them and targeting them with the right messaging. As you create your SaaS product, pay close attention to the features and use cases that make it easier to sell. Work your customer's pain points and your future marketing copy into your application as you go and it will make your job as a salesperson way easier down the road.

Creating Your Minimum Viable Product

Alright, now that's all out of the way we can finally talk about building your product! Don't feel overwhelmed though, you won't be finishing it before you launch.

Wait what?

That's right. First, you want to create what's called a Minimum Viable Product (MVP). This is the minimum amount of features that will provide enough value for a customer to pay for your solution. You may be tempted to build a lot of features, but this will cost you more time and money than just building the bare minimum.

The reason for this is that you will want to release your product as quickly as possible and gather feedback. You can then iterate on the MVP with customer input until it solves their problem, adding more features or changing them if necessary. The idea behind this approach is to minimize time spent building something no one wants while maximizing learning about what people do want.

Aside from the features you know you need, we'll talk about how to actually get the product built and other areas of an application that need to be addressed such as user authentication, flexible pricing, and user experience.

Code vs Low-Code vs No-Code

There are three ways to build a SaaS app: coding, low-code, and no-code. Coding requires programming knowledge but offers the most customization. Low-Code and No-Code solutions are more limited in their capabilities than coding; however, they require less technical expertise or time investment on your part to implement. In this article, we'll explore each of these approaches so you can make an informed decision about which solution will work best for your needs!

First, let's talk about coding. The most basic thing to know is that a SaaS app can be built using code that comes in many different programming languages including PHP, JavaScript, Java, C++, and Python. Code-based solutions are more customizable than other methods of development because you have the power to customize your application as it suits your needs without needing additional work from an engineer or developer. The downside is that this approach requires significant technical knowledge on the part of the programmer; however, learning these skills takes time but once mastered opens up opportunities for building powerful apps with endless customization potentials!

Some examples of great SaaS coding frameworks are:

Express - Express is a minimal and flexible Node.js web application framework, providing a robust set of features for building single as well as multi-page, and hybrid web applications

Symfony - Symfony provides an extensive list of components out-of-the-box to build the full stack with any combination you choose from Full CMS/CRM like functionality (Core), Databases (Doctrine ORM/ODM library), Templating engine (Twig), or even Web server solution that can power your API calls! With all these choices at hand, it becomes much easier to use only what's necessary to get started quickly while maintaining flexibility over time without having to rewrite large parts of code when requirements change.

Laravel - Laravel is a PHP web application framework that provides both the structure and functionality needed for building robust web applications with speed and simplicity. Laravel's Laracasts series has enough video tutorials to teach you everything you need to know to build great web applications.

Django - Python's Django Web framework has been built from the ground up to help developers quickly build reliable, high-performing, public-facing websites. It is an open-source project licensed under Apache License Version two (ASL) which offers free support via our mailing list, IRC channel, or paid commercial support packages.

Low-Code and No-Code approaches offer faster deployment times due to their self-service nature and limited capabilities compared with coding. These options do not allow for a lot of customization but are perfect for prototyping and rapid application development.

No-code solutions offer an off-the-shelf approach to developing apps that require less time, effort, expertise, or money; No code is also typically involved with very little maintenance required once the app has been deployed. Applications developed through this method often have limited functionality which could be its biggest downside depending on your needs!

If you're not trying to code and want to build your own SaaS, tools like these should be first on your list to evaluate:

Bubble.io - Bubble is a web-based platform for prototyping and developing digital products. Bubble lets you build your entire app without having to provision servers or learn complicated development languages.

Wavemaker - Wavemaker is another no-code tool that lets you create a prototype, build and maintain the app. Wavemaker is great for people with limited programming skills or those who are new to coding altogether.

So what should you do? In all seriousness, every company's project requirements will vary so it's best to take some time before making any decisions about which route is right for you.

No code should be your first choice if it's important to get an application up and running quickly without having to learn complex development languages.

User Authentication

As a SaaS app owner, you are responsible for the security of your user's data. One of the easiest ways to do this is by building solid authentication forms into your website. Registration and sign-in forms should have some basic features such as requiring strong passwords (no dictionary words), password requirements, captcha to prevent brute force attacks, and using email instead of username when possible. These simple changes will help keep your user data secure from hackers who want to steal sensitive information like credit card numbers or social security numbers.

"Strong passwords" should have at least one capital letter, number, and special character. It also helps to include a prefix or suffix like an exclamation point for the beginning of your password (e.g., $e4hshbf82axw!). Password requirements can also ensure that people can't use dictionary words when creating passwords which would make them easier targets for brute force attacks. Brute force attacks are when a hacker uses software to automatically try different passwords until the right one is found.

The final step in keeping your user data secure and preventing brute force attacks is using captcha - which are images that someone has to type out or answer correctly before they can proceed with registration or sign-in. Captcha prevents automated programs from trying thousands of passwords per second because humans have an easier time reading them than computers do.

User credentials should never be stored as plain text but rather encrypted where appropriate so hackers can't see it if they manage to break into your database's security. Most programming frameworks handle encrypting your passwords for you using what's known as a "salted hash". A hash is a one-way function that can't be reversed.

A salt is a string of random characters created by combining letters and numbers with no spaces between them, much like passwords are usually composed. The salt can then be combined with the password and hashed to create the salted hash, which is a one-way encryption algorithm and can't be reversed and can be safely stored in your database.

When the user logs in and provides you with their password, add the salt to their input and hash it with the same algorithm you used when you stored it. Then compare the two hashed values. If they are the same, then the password provided is correct.

Another important aspect of user registration/login to consider is the user's ability to reset their password. On the surface, this seems like a simple feature, but you'll need to be able to send emails with unique links in them that are validated on a page on your website that then allows the user to reset their password.

The links in your password reset emails should expire as well, otherwise, they could be accessed at a later time and used to reset the user's password by someone else. 5-10 minutes is usually plenty of time for a password reset link to be used by the intended user. You may think this isn't all necessary at first, but having it will save you on customer support and loads of headache down the road, so better to get it out of the way up front and make your customers happy, right?

Depending on how you are building your product, this is probably all already taken care of by your framework, but I mention it because I see way too many new apps being built and saving plain text passwords to their database. This not only endangers your reputation but could potentially open your users up to identity theft in the case of a data breach.

Choosing Core Features

The first thing that you should do when choosing features for your SaaS MVP is to prioritize solutions to your customers' pain points. The easiest way to find out what the pain points are is by conducting customer interviews and support tickets. If there's a feature that isn't too difficult or time-consuming, then it can be implemented at this point in development before launch. Otherwise, if it's difficult or not vital to the value proposition of your product, wait until after launch so that you have more resources available and don't distract yourself from what really matters—getting initial traction!

To choose which features you should include in your MVP, start by listing out all the features. Next to each feature give it a score from 1-10 for how easy or hard it would be for you to implement with 10 being the easiest and 1 the most difficult. If you're not sure, just make a guess. Now, go through and score them each based on how important they are to your customer with 1 being the least important and 10 being most important. Add the two numbers together and you'll get a quality score for each of your features. Develop those with the highest scores first.

When deciding how many features to add, I like to break things up into stages.

Stage 1: Pre-launch MVP (2 weeks)

This is the stage where you develop and the platform isn't yet ready for customers. Use this time to make the platform ready for customers (ie. registration, login, payment processing, homepage, and some basic features).

Stage 2: Post-Launch MVP (2-6 months)

This is the stage where you are putting on initial customers and collecting feedback. This is when you can really start to develop the meat of your application.

Stage 3: Post-Traction (6-12+ months)

This is when you get to build out all the "nice-to-haves" that haven't been prioritized yet. You have plenty of customers and loads of feedback. Generally, you'll have resources dedicated to the day-to-day and be able to focus on new, creative things you can create.

No one can tell you which features to include in your SaaS product, but that's part of the fun. Try to be smart on where you spend your time since, this early on, every decision you make operates as the fulcrum to your future, with increasingly more impact as time goes on.

Creating a Simple User Interface

There are many ways to design a great user experience, but one of the most important things is simplifying your interface. If you make it too complicated for users, they're going to get frustrated and not be able to use your product. This might sound like common sense, but some companies forget this and end up with an unusable or confusing product that nobody wants.

I was recently working with a company building an online store. They had spent months perfecting the design and look of their website, but they forgot to take into account how easy it was for customers to make actual purchases on the site. There were so many different ways that users could purchase something that most people didn't know which option was best for them. The search filters they worked so hard on barely got noticed.

This led to lots of frustration among shoppers because they couldn't find anything in particular without browsing through all the products available, wasting time and energy. The UI/UX designers realized this problem halfway through production and made changes so that the filters were more prominent on the site and the search functionality was clear to the users.

The changes made to the website's UI/UX gave customers what they wanted: a simple interface that was easy to navigate. Not only were shoppers much more likely to complete their purchase, but those who did have issues with the product found it easier and faster to find help because all of the information about finding a product and how an order is processed can be found easily.

The same holds for every aspect of your interface. You should look at each element that a customer may interact with and ask yourself, "Could this be easier?". If it can, make it easier. Some customers might "get it" how it is today, but will all of them?

Wizards are a great way to help customers get set up. A setup wizard will guide each customer through the process of setting up their account, even if they are a first-time user. Wizards can remove the anxiety a customer may feel with learning and configuring a new piece of software by breaking the configuration down into easy-to-complete steps.

The first thing I would recommend anyone do when looking to simplify your interface is to remove all unnecessary interactions and elements. Try to make every view in your application as basic as possible.

There are three reasons to do this:

- You want to leave room to grow. As you onboard new users, they will request features and changes. If your user interface is complicated, it will be more difficult to accommodate them.
- You want your users to feel confident. It can be confusing for a customer when they are presented with an overwhelming amount of information and choices, especially if they have never used the product before.
- A simple UI will give them a clear path that is easy to follow, decreasing anxiety and frustration levels as well as making it more likely that they will understand how to use your software and stick around.

In your application, you want to make sure you have clear and easy-to-use navigation. Navigation is how your users will get around your app so the simpler it is to find what they're looking for, the more success they will have.

Your user interface can make or break your business. If it's too complicated, customers will churn and you will be left with a ghost town. If it's easy to use, your customer retention rate could be through the roof!

Once you're through the first two weeks, you should have an MVP that people can use and pay for. You've got your core features built and a roadmap to take you through stage 2. Now, you'll need a website so people can find you.

Creating a Website that Converts

It's not enough to have a slick website these days, it needs to convert visitors into customers. For your site to be successful, you need a compelling homepage that grabs the attention of potential customers and gets them excited about your product or service. You also need to take them on a journey by telling them a story as they go through your website.

Sell More Through Storytelling

The story is your most powerful tool in converting visitors into customers. The story is about how the hero (your customer) arrives at success due to the help of their guide (you). You are not the hero in this story - they are.

People remember stories. Why? When we tell a story, our brains activate different regions that would not be activated if it were just facts or data points. The idea of how storytelling is vital to sales may seem like common sense but many companies forget this time-tested principle when designing their marketing message and strategy for their target audience.

Stories last longer in people's mind, so there are less likely to get disconnected from what you're saying before your content has had enough time to sink in and deliver its full value proposition. By using storytelling marketers can create emotions which have been shown by neuroscientists as the key ingredient in creating long-term memories.

People remember stories because they can link different ideas together and make connections between them (which is how we learn) and storytelling creates an emotional connection that increases retention of your message and builds trust with your audience.

If you want to target a specific demographic or psychographic then it's easier for someone who shares these characteristics to understand marketing messages when framed as a story rather than just facts or figures since not everyone perceives data the same way.

Finally - there's some evidence from neuroscience research that the brain is hardwired for storytelling - I won't spend time on it here, but check out the Journal of Neuroscience for more details on how the brain is wired for this learning method.

Features vs Benefits

Use the pain point interview responses you have to identify the pain points your app can solve. There may be a few you didn't realize you were solving in the process! Take these pain points and attribute them to features. Then determine what the benefit to the user is from that feature and use that on your website.

For instance, if the user's pain point is that their bakery is suffering due to low foot traffic in their store, you might have a feature that notifies customers of 24 hours sales, leading them to come into the store. You wouldn't list this on your website as "Sales Notifications". Instead, describe it as "Increase foot traffic in your store". This keeps the customer from having to connect the dots in their mind and, instead, presents them with the result (and benefit to them) immediately.

Here are a few more examples:

Feature: Directory of real estate agents
Benefit: Find a home that is perfect for you and your family

Feature: Dark mode now available
Benefit: Use your phone in bed without disturbing those around you

Feature: Control the app with your voice
Benefit: Stay safer on the road with voice control

What's the point? The point is that you have a lot more power to motivate customers into action than you may realize. Conversion rates are often much higher when there is an emotional component in play or where trust has been established with credibility promises and social proof. You also get better conversion rates if your visitors feel like their needs, identities, beliefs, values or emotions have been validated.

Homepage

Your homepage is ground zero for conversion rate optimization. Make sure you spend some extra time here to put your best foot forward with new prospects. You also need to have a clear and compelling offer and you should be telling them what they are going to get as soon as possible.

Your homepage needs to tell the visitor that it's about this one thing, not everything under the sun. It also has to present immediate value before asking for contact information or anything like that. If you need to list out a bunch of benefits (notice I didn't say "features") then create a secondary page that lists out the benefits to the customer with a short explanation of each.

The more you can niche down in the language you use, the better. For instance, if your customers are bakers, then use phrases like "Sweeten the deal", instead of "Get a discount" with headlines like "The best POS system for bakers who rock". - be specific to your niche. You want the customer to feel like you are speaking directly to them every step of the way, holding their hand, not standing on a stage speaking to a crowd.

About Page

Your website also needs an About page so people know who you are and why they should trust you with their money when buying products or services from you. They'll want to know more about who's running things too - having pictures of all team members on the About Page will help reassure potential customers that there are actually real people behind this business!

When you're coming up with the copy for your about page, think about what you're trying to tell customers. What is your story? Why should customers relate to you and want to work with you?

The about page is your chance to make your business feel more human by showcasing how human you are. If you're building this thing by yourself, don't be afraid to say so. Be honest and transparent.

Pricing Page

On your pricing page, you'll want to showcase your plans and include a frequently asked questions section at the bottom to answer questions that the customer may be thinking about when they are considering purchasing.

These, at a minimum, should include:

· What happens if I exceed my plan limits?
· How do I get a refund?
· Is there a credit card required for the free trial?
· Is there a commitment or can I cancel at any time?

When you display your plans to the customer, the natural inclination is to display them from left to right going from lowest cost to highest cost. But if you flip it around, you'll actually get more customers paying for more expensive plans. This is called "Price Anchoring".

Price anchoring is a marketing technique of showing a product at an initially high price and then reducing the initial cost so that the consumer perceives it as a better value than if they saw only one price.

You're essentially presenting the customer with the highest price first so they perceive your product as more valuable. This makes every other plan seem cheaper than if they had seen the least expensive plan first.

It's subtle psychology but it works to not only get people on higher-level plans but also increases conversion overall since your product will be seen as more valuable.

Terms of Service & Privacy Policy

If you want to really establish trust with a visitor to your site, ensure you have a terms of service and privacy policy linked to in the footer of every page. This is the bare minimum for any business on the internet and, if it's missing, people won't trust that your business is legit.

You probably don't need to hire a lawyer and pay a ton to get these written. Hiring a lawyer to write your terms of service can easily run you $10-20k. Instead, get on Google and find a "SaaS Terms of Service Generator" that will work. They are usually free or very cheap and will ask you a series of questions about your website - do you use cookies, what liabilities do you have, etc. Then you'll get concise terms of use you can use until you start bringing in the big bucks and can hire a lawyer to write you a bespoke document.

What About Social Proof?

Social proof is a huge indicator of credibility. The concept of social proof is widely used in marketing, and it's a powerful way to get people interested in your products. Social proof is the idea that when people see other people doing something they are more likely to do it themselves.

You can tell someone about how great something tastes or you could have them watch somebody else enjoying said thing on YouTube. When customers see others using your product or service or hear them talk positively about their experiences, they may be more inclined to use it themselves because those around them are having a positive outcome and people naturally make decisions based on what other people around them like.

In the real world, social proof might work like this:

Aimee was scrolling through her Facebook newsfeed and stopped to read the following post from one of her favorite bloggers, Sarah.

"I just posted my latest project on Pinterest! I also made a few pins for recipes that are easy, healthy, and delicious! This is fun!"

She felt connected to Sarah's story because she loved all of those qualities in food as well and also created art projects from time to time. Aimee then wanted to see what else Sarah was up to on Pinterest, so she signed up for her own account.

Now Aimee is a Pinterest user as well and can post her own projects and recipes. This all happened with zero cost to Pinterest. The social proof of Sarah's post drew Aimee in organically.

Social proof doesn't have to be on social media though. In fact, it should be all over your website. Social proof is powerful enough that you can safely drop it in just about any section of your website and it will have a net positive effect.

Third-party testimonials, social media shares, and positive reviews all help potential customers feel confident about buying from your business. The problem is, you likely don't have any social proof yet.

Fixing that is easy, but takes a little time. The first thing you need is happy customers. Then, all you need to do is ask them for their testimonials, post them on your website. Once you get your first customers, make sure to get testimonials from them and get them on your website as quickly as possible.

Tip: If you want a double whammy, when you ask them for a review, point them to your profile on G2 and have them leave the review there. That way you get a public review on G2 to help your presence there and you get the testimonial you can use on your website.

Generating Traffic

Generating initial traffic for your SaaS product can be tough. If you've built up a social audience, that can be a great springboard to get your first users. Your first users are the most important since they will be providing you with your initial feedback to improve the product and user experience for future users. Pulling these people in from your existing network means they will be more forthcoming with their feedback.

To generate traffic, you need a plan for how and where people are going to hear about it. There's no "silver bullet" solution that works equally well for everyone - each business has different needs when it comes to marketing strategy. But there is one fundamental principle of marketing: The more exposure the better! And this can be achieved by using both traditional methods such as broadcasting on major news networks (if you've got the budget!) as well as newer methods like leveraging social media communities (e.g., Facebook groups).

Creating a Blog

Creating a blog is also a must-have for a SaaS business. Your blog, paired with good SEO practices, can be a traffic generator for your business for years into the future. The time and/or money invested in content today will retain its value more than any paid ad campaign could. The best part about traffic to your blog is that it's free and has limitless potential. Organic traffic is the highest converting, most engaged traffic you can get.

When deciding what topics to cover in your blog, you should first think about your customers and what they want to learn about. See, the goal here is for potential customers to search google for a topic that's related to your business and for you to provide the answer. For instance, if your application helps businesses with their accounting, writing blog articles with tips on how to do your own accounting will attract people who need your help.

You might be thinking "But why would I give away my secrets for free?". The answer is two-fold:

1.) By writing about how you do what you do, you show your would-be customers how knowledgeable you are. This can help qualify you when they do decide they need someone's help.

2.) Your blog readers associate you with solutions to their problems. This means your blog can be building trust in you with your potential customers while you're sleeping.

Don't worry too much about stuffing keywords in your content or getting too scientific with your post topics. Instead, be genuine and try to provide real value to your readers. If you want to do anything to target search engines, the only thing I would focus on is making sure your posts are at least 1,000 words long.

If you're not much of a writer and have some extra cash on hand, you can hire a writer to write for you. You don't need a full-time employee for this. Instead, check out services like Verblio, where you can post a request and writers will fulfill it with original content you buy the rights to. You can usually get 1,000-word posts written for about $100-150 each.

Search Engine Optimization

While the content you write should be targeted at people instead of search engines, the HTML structure of your website is another story. You want to make sure you have best practices implemented so that your data is structured for search engines to easily absorb and classify.

Personally, I like to use WordPress for my public-facing website, even if my app is built on another platform. WordPress has some great SEO plugins and is pretty good on its own without any modifications. There is also a ton of documentation and forums posts about SEO on WordPress and how you can optimize it. I won't get into the nitty-gritty of coding SEO practices as those change frequently, but if you go with a proven CMS like WordPress, you'll have to do a lot less discovery on your own.

Getting your website's HTML dialed for SEO can make all the efforts on your blog work 100x for you. The combination of good coding practices (as far as SEO is concerned) along with valuable content, posted regularly, can get organic traffic flowing into your website much quicker than it would otherwise.

At any rate, don't expect SEO to drive much traffic for at least the first 6-12 months. As you continue to keep creating content, it will continue to get indexed, casting more lines out to see to catch some potential customers.

App Marketplaces

Another way to acquire users for free is to integrate with an existing marketplace. Platforms like Shopify, Salesforce, and BigCommerce have marketplaces with apps their customers can install and use to extend their software offerings. Integrating your SaaS into one of these platforms could mean money in the bank if the app resonates with the user base.

It's important to remember that all apps won't work on all platforms. For instance, just because a project management app might work as an extension of Salesforce, doesn't mean e-commerce store owners on Shopify would want to use it and pay for it. If your app is a good fit, it can do really well in a marketplace - especially if you find a usability gap that's not being met by other apps or the host platform. If your app isn't a good fit, then you likely won't see any users come from your effort.

You can evaluate the desire for your app by looking at the individual app stores at apps like yours and checking out their reviews. Reviews will help you identify shortcomings in those apps that you might be able to solve.

Build your integration and submit your app. Generally, once approved, customers will start trickling in. Then, you pay the host platform a commission on the revenue from the customers they sent you. It's a little restrictive, but can be a great revenue driver in the early stages of your business.

Helping Other People

Each time you post something online - a blog post, a social post, a comment - anything, you get exposure. Use this to your advantage. Find where your target customers are and start engaging them, answering their questions, and helping them when they need it. Don't sell them your product, just make yourself available.

Obviously, you can find people on social media. Reddit in particular has many subreddits dedicated to niches that might share an audience with yours. Reddit has some strict spam policies, so make sure you don't sell on there, but as long as you are providing genuine value you shouldn't have any issues.

Another great forum for helping your would-be customers is Quora. People come to Quora to ask all kinds of questions. Search for people asking questions related to your niche and answer them. Your description next to your avatar can tell them about your product, so use the opportunity to be as helpful as possible.

When you help other people online, it not only provides initial interaction with potential customers, but it sticks around, solidifying your reputation as an authority in your industry. Someone may be searching for answers to the same problem at a later time and your previous efforts will draw them in as well.

Automating Email Outreach

If you're running your business as a solopreneur or small team, every minute of your day is important. You need to automate as much as you can so you can focus on building your business and closing sales. One of the easiest and most effective things you can automate in your business is email communication with prospects and customers.

Automating email can bring in warm leads and keep customers coming back for more. As long as you keep an eye on your deliverability and sender reputation, cold emails follow-up campaigns and nurturing sequences can help supercharge your business while you focus on more pressing issues at hand like helping existing customers and adding new features.

Understanding Deliverability

Your email campaigns will only be effective, though, if they land in the recipient's inbox. Email service providers (ESPs) have tons of checks in place to detect spam prevent it from reaching its destination. So how do you avoid being flagged as spam?

Email deliverability is all about the sender's reputation. If you have a bad sender reputation, your emails will be blocked or filtered out before they arrive in an inbox. If you have a good reputation, your emails will be delivered as expected.

If you want to avoid being flagged as spam and maintain a good sender reputation with ESPs then it's important that:

- You use clean IP addresses for sending email campaigns (either by using your own server or outsourced)
- Ensure your domain name is not on any blacklists
- Avoid profanity and messages that only contain images
- Warm-up your email address domain and IPs

Warming up your email domain is an important pre-emptive measure to make sure your email domain is not blacklisted.

Warming Up Your IP/Domain

Warming up an IP address means sending a small number of emails from it to get the recipient on the other end's whitelist. This way, when you send out a larger campaign in the future, they will be less likely to flag your messages as spam and more likely that you'll reach their destination.

Once you've warmed up your IP addresses or domains then following these best practices for content:

- Be professional with copy (no exclamation marks!)

- Keep subject lines concise so ESPs can easily scan them quickly
- Use bullet points instead of paragraphs if possible
- Include links only where necessary (only provide links to content on your website)
- Keep the body of your email succinct
- Include a call to action at the end (like subscribe, share with friends/colleagues, sign up for a webinar, etc.)

After that is taken care of you can start automating outreach campaigns. You'll need to work out an automated cold email sequence based on relevant pain points in the customer's journey.

Unsubscribe Links

Another thing you must have is an unsubscribe link. Unsubscribe links are important because there is a chance people will not want to hear from you anymore and this way they can stop. Also, there are regulatory reasons to include an unsubscribe link in the footer of all automated messages. The CANSPAM Act of 2003 requires all commercial emails in the United States to contain an unsubscribe link, which allows recipients the opportunity to opt-out of future emails. It also requires that a physical address for the sender be present.

Here's a rundown of the basic CANSPAM requirements:

- Don't falsify your email headers
- Don't use deceptive subject lines
- Identify your message as an ad
- Include your physical address (P.O. Boxes are fine)

- Include an unsubscribe link
- Honor unsubscribes within 10 days
- Monitor what others do on your behalf

That last one is important. If you hire a freelancer to help you with your email marketing, you are responsible for what they send out on your behalf. You need to make sure you know what emails are going out from your business. The fines for violating CANSPAM in the US can be north of $40k *per violation*!

Cold Email Sequences

You can also automate cold email sequences to go out to potential prospects to find people who need your product. Automated cold emails can land you in the spam folder if you're not careful so it's somewhat of an art.

The most important rule of automating cold emails is don't make them look automated. This is the quickest way to get ignored. Instead, include some basic personalization, like the person's name.

Don't include their job title or other info as this is normally not something you'd type out (ie. CEO of The Company and Fun Dad). Instead, keep the emails short and to the point.

Also, don't include bullet points and any other formatting. Just type out what's on your mind for this particular person. Don't worry about getting the perfect pitch just yet – that will come later in the process.

For example: *Hi Rebecca! I noticed we're both from Oregon, so wanted to say hi :) What are you up to these days?*

While it may seem like an over-the-top idea at first glance, with how many emails people receive every day, personalizing an email can be enough "to grab their attention" (AKA make them open my message). The key is not including too much information or trying too hard - instead keep things short and prompt for a response - this will start a conversation that can lead to a sale.

But where do you get leads? For B2B products, LinkedIn can be a great place. There are a lot of businesses that will "rent" you access to their database of leads for SaaS businesses. Growbots, for instance, does this. With Growbots, you can target specific industries and send emails from the same platform - this can keep your marketing IPs sparkly clean even if your cold campaign turns south.

Follow-up Emails

Automated follow-up emails are a great way to increase the likelihood of conversion. These are emails that you set up in advance and they're triggered after a certain amount of time has passed or maybe when someone doesn't open your initial email.

The most common follow-up campaign is one where it prompts them for their phone number or to schedule a 1:1 call. Taking it a step further than the original message, this shows you are focused on them and would like to have a genuine engagement.

Nurturing Campaigns

Nurturing campaigns are used to keep in touch with prospects who have shown some interest but haven't made a purchase yet, or maybe you want to send them a discount code for their birthday. You can also provide content from your blog, free resources, or link to other websites that you think your customers would find valuable.

The purpose of nurturing campaigns is to stay top of mind for your customers and prospects. Each time you send an email, you remind them you exist and you are here to solve their problems (without actually saying it, of course!).

Nurturing Campaign Ideas:

Content Sharing - you can share posts from your blog or other content that could be relevant to your audience. For instance, in the tutorial business, a customer may find an article on how to fix a leaky faucet interesting and useful because they have just gone through this experience themselves. You are not trying to sell anything with these emails but rather offer helpful resources for them or their friends/family members who might need it!

Coupons - if there is ever something special going on at your business, like Black Friday sales starting early then you will want to send out promotional codes to the subscribers on your email list so they get access before everyone else does. They would also appreciate coupon codes for their birthday.

Product updates - if you have a new product coming out, people on your email list would appreciate knowing about it before everyone else does.

They might want to buy one right away and will be excited when they see the update in their inbox because they know there is something good coming soon!

While it takes some planning to get everything set up, you can imagine with automated systems working for you and maintaining customer relationships, you'll be able to not only focus on the core of your business but grow faster than you could on your own, sending messages manually.

Generating Leads

A lead magnet is a marketing technique that you can use to attract potential customers. They are typically free, valuable content or software that visitors can download straight away. Lead magnets allow you to build an email list of people who have shown interest in your product and will hopefully convert into paying customers at some point.

I recommend starting with a lead magnet that is related to your SaaS product. You might have created some unique content or collected some insights from customers about insights in their markets, for example. Package this up in a way you can offer it as a free download for others to consume. Make sure you brand it with your SaaS brand.

Collecting Leads

Create a landing page where people can sign up by giving their email address in return for access to the download. Once someone has signed up, they'll be added to your list of potential customers who are more likely to convert than someone who isn't interested in the content you have.

The key here is to make sure what you're offering is in line with your main product so you attract the right people.

MicroSaaS as a Lead Magnet

A lead magnet can also be another SaaS product. MicroSaaS products make great lead magnets since you can develop a simple tool to give away for free in exchange for someone's email address.

For instance, if you have a B2B email marketing platform, you could offer an email list scrubber tool that would clean lists for businesses. The benefit to the business is that their lists stay clean and it gives you something you can give away to potential clients to start a conversation with them.

A lead magnet could also be an e-book, whitepaper, webinar, or video. The key is to offer something of value that you can give away for free and then use the subsequent email conversations as a way to promote your main product.

Once someone accepts the offer for your lead magnet, you should add them to your automated nurturing campaign and outbound sales emails. This way, you continue to provide them value while also contacting them with an offer for your primary product.

Partnerships

Partnering with other apps and organizations can be a great source of leads for your business. Many businesses will refer people to you for nothing in return, just because they can help out their customers! For those who don't, you can pay a commission for each customer they send your way. Balance it out by making the deal both ways and you earn a commission for referring customers to them too!

The best partnership deals involve getting your app worked into the customer onboarding flow of another, related SaaS product or newsletter. This way, there is a steady stream of people being exposed to your app and you're able to grow alongside your partner. This way too, you ensure that your app is part of the ecosystem with your partner app. People who use both together will discuss it on forums and social media, giving you more social proof and word-of-mouth referrals than you would have gotten on your own.

Other partnerships may involve sending out email blasts from time to time. In these cases, you can expect to receive a boost of traffic upfront, but that will quickly taper off. If your partner has a large audience, this could be good exposure and acquisition, however, you will need to keep looking for new ways to generate leads after the initial traction fades.

Running Demos

Every salesperson knows that software demos are an important part of the sales process. Software demos allow you to learn more about your prospect, demonstrate your software, answer questions and ease any concerns they may have.

A well-conducted demo can be a great success for both parties, but it's important to make sure that the demo is as efficient as possible so you get the most out of your limited time with the customer. It can be helpful to send the customer some questions via email or online survey ahead of time so you can prepare better for the meeting. Booking software like Calendly will let you ask these questions when they are scheduling their demo.

Don't start a demo with an explanation of what your company does. This will bore the customer and they'll tune out from listening to you, even if it is relevant. Instead, introduce yourself and engage in small talk for two minutes before starting on a software demonstration. You can use this time to learn more about the person's interests or hobbies so that you know how to tailor your presentation later.

After the initial introduction, set the expectations for the meeting by going over the agenda. This way, you can ensure everyone is on the same page before you start and, if there is anything the customer wants to add to the agenda, you can make sure you factor in time for their request.

Sample Agenda (30 min meeting)

1. Introductions (1-2 min)
2. Set expectations, go over agenda (2 min)
3. Go over customer's answers to your survey (5 min)
4. Present the value proposition (the "what" and "why") (3 min)
5. Plans, costs, etc. (Offer a special deal) (3 min)
6. Software Demo (10 min)
7. Q & A (5 min)

After setting expectations and covering the agenda, thank them for answering the questions in advance and go over the answers to their questions with them. This you an opportunity to get clarity on anything that requires further explanation as well as allows them to amend to change their responses.

Now that the formalities are out of the way, you should follow with your product's value proposition. Explain to them what your mission is, why you do what you do, how you can help them, how you've helped other people like them and why the cost for your product is justified. Being able to show them a positive ROI as an example at this stage can help get their mind in the right place for the next stage of the demo.

Now that you've shown them how valuable your product is and why you are the company that does it exactly how they need, hit them with costs. Show them a couple of different pricing options. You could present them with monthly and annual pricing, but also throw in a 3-month deal that has a discount vs going month to month - something that's not available on your website that this is their first encounter with. This increases the sense of urgency while giving them an out if they are more price-sensitive, while still landing you the sale.

Now it's time to show them the product.

Present information logically by guiding them through screens one at a time, showing each new feature as it comes up rather than throwing all features together into one big mess because not everyone has perfect recall like computers do! It's important to also limit demos to no more than fifteen minutes to give enough time afterward for any questions that arise during the presentation.

You should know, at this point, which features would be most important to them. Start with these and don't worry about showing off every single thing the product does. If you run out of time, you can always mention there are other great features they should check out when they sign up

IDEA TO ACQUISITION

for a trial!

Running a great demo isn't hard if you have the right structure in place. You'll find customers appreciate the efficiency and it really comes across as representing your business in the best light.

At the end of the demo, make sure you have established the "next steps" with the customer. Either they are going to do something, you are going to do something, or you'll be having a follow-up call later. Regardless, go ahead and put a time and date to it to keep things moving. It's up to you to keep up the pace and close the deal, so don't be afraid to get another call on the calendar before you sign off.

108

Optimizing Customer Onboarding

Customer onboarding is the key to success for any SaaS. Once you have a customer, the most important thing is to get them to the "Aha!" moment as soon as they sign up, meaning that you need to show them how the product solves their problem quickly and efficiently.

Just like with any business strategy, there are many different ways of doing it well - but no matter which one you choose it is important that your experience is personalized and dynamic.

Leave the Heavy Lifting to Your App

With high-ticket sales, onboarding can consist of multiple meetings with different people from each company, loads of paperwork and red tape, and months-long sales cycles. Most SaaS apps aren't high-ticket for their ideal customer though. This means that your onboarding process takes place primarily inside your software.

The more that you can leave the heavy lifting to your app during onboarding, the more you can create a repeatable process for signing up and activating new customers. This is imperative if you want to scale to thousands of new users every month. The team you would need to support high-touch customers with those numbers would drive the business into the red. But with a streamlined, software-based onboarding approach, you are only limited by your ability to reach new customers.

Registration

Your registration form should be as simple as possible. I normally only have the name, email, and password fields. No need to split up the name into two fields - for most people you can do this later programmatically. There's also no need to make them repeat their password. As long as you have a reset password link on your login page, they will be able to gain access to their account.

The registration page shouldn't have any sort of navigation on it other than maybe a link to go to the login page if they already have an account and ended up there. You can also make your logo clickable to go back to the homepage, but that's it. If someone has made it to this point in your funnel, you want them focused specifically on the task at hand - signing up for your product.

Each form field that you require your users to fill out will reduce your conversion rate. If you wanted to take it a step further, you could allow users to sign up using only their email address or phone number. Then you could have them provide more information such as password, name, etc on a secondary step after they create their account. If you include this information as part of a setup wizard, you can segue them into completing their account setup.

Account Setup Wizard

The first step after registration is getting the customer through a setup wizard or showing them a checklist of steps to complete now that they have an account. Personalize the experience to them and call them by name to make it feel like you are talking one-on-one with your customer.

By breaking their setup process down into easy-to-complete steps, you increase the chances of them completing it and they will appreciate the effort that went into making the process easy for them.

Users on the internet, by default, just don't want to set things up or fill out forms - they just want stuff to work. Try to make it "just work" as best you can and remove any unnecessary steps that can be completed at a later time.

During the setup wizard, make sure you display the number of steps left vs the number completed. This can help users get an idea of what's left and can ease their minds if they are thinking this will be a cumbersome process.

When the setup wizard is complete, congratulate them within the user interface! People release dopamine when someone congratulates them and it makes them associate completing the account set up with a positive experience.

Personalize Your UI

Dynamic text in your user interface is a great way of making the experience even more personalized - for example, when someone hits the dashboard, you could display some text that says "Good Afternoon, John" where John is the user and the greeting is based on his timezone. This can be a friendly way to connect with users and relieve their anxiety caused by learning a new product.

That's really what onboarding is all about - relieving the customer's anxiety about your product and showing them how easy it is to solve their pain.

A quality of life addition you could make to your app is to take all features that could be considered moderately confusing or difficult to any of your users and disable them on new accounts by default, leaving only the easiest-to-use features.

During the setup wizard, prompt the user with a question about how they will use the software and enable any relevant features for them. This can help if your app does a lot, but many users only use a specific subset of your features. Put the rest as an "advanced setting" in case customers want to enable anything not yet shown in their account.

Monitor User Behavior & Remove Friction

As people sign up to use your product, you should monitor their behavior as best you can. Tools like Hotjar can give you insights into where people are getting confused with your interface and Google Analytics can show you where they are bouncing if they get frustrated.

By identifying bottlenecks in the user experience, you can systematically attack each one, one at a time, to ease users into the application more smoothly.

A prime example of a bottleneck I see often is making your customers choose a plan and enter their credit card at signup. The common behavioral pattern in this scenario is that most users sign up, then, when presented with no other option than to supply payment information, simply leave, never to return.

This prevents them from experiencing the software completely, and definitely keeps them away from the "Aha!" you want them to experience.

Instead, a better way to approach it is to drop the user straight into the application on a timed trial or with some features disabled until they supply payment information. You can then display this message at the top of each page in the application.

The user now will be able to experience your app, albeit with limited functionality, but still get the "Aha!" moment where everything clicks and they decide they want to do business.

Removing friction in the signup process will optimize the odds that a new user will become your customer. Remember, it's better to gather data and act than to make assumptions, so you should sign up for your own app regularly and experience your onboarding process for yourself - try to do this from the perspective of your customers.

Mastering Customer Support

What do you get when you combine the best product in your industry with the best customer support? You get a SaaS business that is unstoppable. The most successful SaaS businesses have mastered customer support. It's not just about creating great documentation for your product, it's about assisting your customers through every step of their journey with you. In SaaS, you don't sell software, you sell support.

Customer support starts with your user interface. If your interface isn't clear, then customers will have questions. The best way to keep your interface easily understood is by keeping it simple. But if you need to have more complex explanations, link to simple and concise documentation.

Step-by-Step Documentation

Your customers need to know how to use your product, and they also want it to do everything that you promised them when you convinced them of its value in your marketing materials. Documenting how to set up, configure and use each feature of your application will let your customers find answers for themselves. When you are a small team, you want customers to email you with new or unique questions, but not with the same questions over and over.

Support Emails & Helpdesk Software

Keeping track of support emails is a must and can become a huge problem as you scale. While using your regular inbox will work at first, when your team is fielding 50-100+ support tickets per day you'll wish you had started with a better system in place.

Helpdesk software like Intercom, Zendesk, and HelpScout are made for this, but can be pretty pricey - there are lots, so shop around. Helpdesk software lets you communicate with your customers via email and live chat all from within your browser. You can connect multiple team members and track conversations in threads easily. When a customer's problem has been solved, you can close the ticket and move on.

It's important to stay organized with your customer support tickets or you could have upset customers who want to leave. Don't believe me? Think about the last time you had to call the support line for your cable company!

Try to respond to live chats within 60 seconds and emails within 2 hours during business hours or 24 hours on holidays and weekends. If you wait too long to respond to a customer, they could cancel their account before you have a chance.

Addressing Customer Complaints

When you do have a customer complaint, address it immediately. Most of the time, your customers aren't going to be mad at you, they are just having a problem that needs to be addressed.

It could be that they aren't using the software correctly. In this case, you need to point them to the step-by-step docs or update your docs to alleviate the confusion. If there is a bug, get it patched as quickly as you can. Use this as an opportunity to turn the customer's negative experience into a positive experience.

Because your customer is having a problem with your software that is frustrating to them, they are more engaged than usual. Use this opportunity to treat them well and demonstrate that you are there for them in a time of need. Solve the problem, apologize, offer them something for their trouble. Some of the best customers I've ever had started as a problem ticket.

Handling Feature Requests

Your customers will also ask for new features. These might be additional functionality, and integration with a particular software they use or just something they think would be cool. Ultimately it's at your discretion which of these you will pursue and which you will not. I like to use the rule that if 5 people asked for it, then it goes on the roadmap. If 10 people ask, then it's next in line.

As you get more customers, you'll get more feature requests. Many of them will only come from one person and be super specific to their use case. You can't spend your time developing features that only one customer will use, so you need to figure out a system to prioritize.

You do this by looking at the number of people making a request, but also how many have made similar requests. The more customers that are asking for something, and the more it's on-trend with what others want to see from you, then the higher priority it has in your development queue.

While you're not able to include all customer feedback into future releases because of scope limitations - which is going to be an ongoing challenge as you grow- every new release should include some features based on customer feature suggestions. Showing customers that you listen will keep the feedback coming and lower churn.

Fixing Bugs With Grace

It's not uncommon for a customer to contact you with something that they think is wrong. When you're able to quickly identify and fix the problem, it can save your relationship with customers - which is worth way more than whatever time went into fixing the bug in the first place. Bugs happen all of the time in software development, but how you react when one comes across your desk makes all the difference.

Bugs can pop up for several reasons. Here are some of the most common types of bugs you may encounter:

- **Functional** - Functional bugs are problems where something in the app isn't working as expected. This could be something like a search input not returning any results.

- **Performance** - Performance bugs are generally inefficient scripts or processes that are slow to execute like a slow loading page or memory leak.
- **Usability** - Usability bugs are places where friction is introduced in your interface to the point that most users don't understand what they should do.
- **Compatibility** - Compatibility bugs are related to integrations between your app and 3rd-party apps. These can happen for many reasons like if the 3rd-party updates their API or data structures.
- **Security** - Security bugs are vulnerabilities in your app that hackers can exploit. These types of bugs are the most critical since they can jeopardize your system and your customers' data.

You shouldn't beat yourself up over bugs. Try to avoid them, but get used to them. The more you work on your app, the higher the likelihood that you'll introduce new bugs.

When a customer reports a bug to you - especially if the issue impacts them significantly - you should respond quickly and apologize for the inconvenience.

Then, fix it asap! You can't make everyone happy all of the time but fixing bugs after they've been reported will go a long way in saving your reputation with your customers.

When I'm building an app or making changes to one that already exists, my priority is always to find any potential problems before releasing anything new onto production servers. This gives me peace of mind knowing that no surprises are waiting for our users once they encounter something wrong on their devices.

Finally, try not to send out mass emails (or other communications) about every little bug report, but do send out a few to keep customers in the loop.

The more responsive and transparent you are when dealing with bugs in production code - no matter how small or large they may be - the better off your app is going to fare long term. Keep in mind: The ugly truth is that even if we fix all our bugs today, there's still tomorrow for new problems to arise!

Raising Money From Investors

Raising funding for your startup might be the right choice if it's starting to take off. Although I recommend you wait as long as possible before your raise, as waiting may give your company more time to grow and build a sustainable business, without the need for outside funding. However, there are many valid reasons to bring on investors early in a startup's life cycle.

Negotiating With Investors

Investors can provide important mentorship and connections, as well as offer funding in the form of a loan or an equity investment. In many cases, investors are looking for exposure to innovative ideas with high potential upside. The downside is they often take a large piece of your company's ownership (often 20-25% of the company).

The key to negotiating terms with investors is understanding what you're getting into, and knowing what your goals are. If your startup has a lot of demonstrable traction such as significant revenue or user acquisition, then it's more likely that investors would be willing to take a smaller stake in the company.

If you want investors to be active hands-on participants, they'll need more of a say and will require additional equity ownership from founders.

The other thing is that when negotiating terms with an investor, the founder needs to have a reasonable exit strategy should things not work out as planned. This could be a strategic partnership, an acquisition, or simply having the option to return capital that isn't invested back to investors with interest.

Types of Investors

In a perfect world, founders would be able to find investors that align with their values, goals, and vision. However, this is often not the case so it's important for entrepreneurs to at least understand what they're getting into when they enter these negotiations.

There are two types of investors you'll likely encounter at this stage.

- **Venture Capitalists** - Venture capitalists ("VCs") are usually investing in new and emerging companies. They generally invest by purchasing equity shares of a company to provide funding for the business ($1M+ investment)
- **Angel Investors** - Angel investors ("Angels") are typically investing in early-stage firms intending to achieve high returns. They invest by purchasing equity shares or convertible debt at smaller amounts than VCs. (< $1M investments)

Do you really need the money?

It's important to realize that, although increased capital is coming into the business, the investor likely won't want you to pay yourself from it, so you need to have a clear reason to raise if you are giving up equity and/or control of your business.

Before you raise money for your business ask yourself the following questions:

- What do I need the money for?
- How much do I really need?
- Can this be done for less?
- Is this vital to the business?

If you don't have a clear idea of where each dollar will go, you probably shouldn't raise it at this stage.

Valid reasons to raise would be:

- Hiring employees to help you with an increasing workload
- Upgrading servers to handle increased traffic
- Licensing software needed for your core value prop
- Paying for legal documents you need to sign a large deal

Remember, too, that the goal is to sell this business in the end. Any equity you give up to an investor is less money you'll have after a sale (unless, of course, it's necessary to raise as stated above) and you won't have the final say in the selling price along with the freedom to negotiate with your future buyer.

The investor may call off a deal they think is too small that you might have been happy with. I've done it both ways and there are pros and cons to each. If you're in doubt about whether or not you should raise money, then you shouldn't.

Creating a Pitch Deck & Executive Summary

If you do decide to raise money from investors, you'll need a pitch deck and an executive summary. A pitch deck is typically a PowerPoint presentation or PDF document that outlines your company's business model, strategy, and financials. The executive summary is a document that basically says the same thing as your pitch deck but in much, much more detail. The purpose of both of them is to convince investors that your business is worth their money.

Your pitch deck should be compelling and succinct, with clear call-to-actions for potential investors to take the next steps. It's a good idea to include at least one visual in your presentation (e.g., an infographic). You'll want the visuals you use in your presentation to tell a story, so your presentation is not just about numbers.

The first step to creating a pitch deck is outlining the content and structure of your presentation. You'll want to include specific information like:

- The problem you're solving with your business (e.g., "we have created an app that helps people find good deals when shopping online.")
- The solution you're providing to the problem (e.g., "we design our app in a way that makes it easy for people to find discounts.")

- How much money your company is generating and how quickly that number will grow over time ("our projected revenue by 2025 is $100 million")
- Next steps for your investors to take

Investors are generally very busy, but not uninterested. After all, investing is how they make their money so most will check out a pitch deck or executive summary if presented the opportunity and the idea sounds good on the surface.

Craft your pitch deck to be entertaining, informative, and *extremely succinct*. Trim as much fat as you can from it to make it only the most vital information. Zuora has a famous pitch deck you can find online with a Google search that has been dubbed the "best pitch deck of all time" or something like that. Search around and take a look at what other brands are doing and you'll get a good idea of what you need to hold your own alongside them.

Your executive summary should lay out everything anyone would ever need to know about your business. The backstory, the financials, the team, where you're going in the future, the state of your market now, the state of the market in 10 years - literally everything there is to say about your business should be in this document. At the end, put how much you are raising, a detailed breakdown on where the money will be spent, and your contact information if they want to invest.

Spending time creating the pitch deck, the executive summary, and chasing down investors for meetings can be a full-time job all on its own. If it's needed, then it's time well spent. Otherwise, that's the time your competitors have been working on their apps while you were distracted by shiny things.

Selling Your Business

Selling your SaaS business may seem like a daunting task, but it doesn't have to be. If you're thinking about selling your SaaS company then there are some things that you will need to prepare for before going through the process of finding a buyer and negotiating a deal. Organize all of the assets from your company and separate personal accounts and login credentials from those belonging to the business itself so you know what is being sold with the sale and remember – *the real value is the amount someone is willing to pay!*

Preparing Your Assets

After only a few months of running a SaaS platform, you probably have all kinds of accounts, logins, and assets related to your business. Hopefully, you've kept these separate from your personal accounts because the first thing you need to do to sell is to isolate everything you can from other business and personal accounts you may have.

When selling your business, you want everything to go as smoothly as possible. That means pre-packing the business to sell. Think about it like this – if you were selling a car, would it make sense to list it for sale while it's still missing a steering wheel that you're using in your other car? Of course not. Even if you told the potential buyers that you'll buy a new steering wheel for it when they buy it, it's not gonna cut it.

Selling software is the same way. People want to know the transition will go smoothly. So when a potential buyer says, "What's involved with the transition?", you want to be able to reply, "Everything is ready to go, I just need to share the logins and have you update the credits card on any paid services". That will instill confidence in the buyer and, when the time comes to actually transfer the assets, you'll be able to do it in a few minutes without much hassle at all.

Calculating Your Value

Once this is done, figure out how much your company is worth. A lot of this really comes down to your revenue and the growth that you've had since you started the business. To get a realistic idea of what you could expect to sell for, take the revenue you've made over the past 12 months and multiply it by 3. This is how much you could logically argue your company is worth. The 3 represents the next 3 years what the buyer would make from running the business as it stands today.

12 mo. Revenue x 3 = Valuation

I generally use this as a bottom line. That would be the least you should accept. It doesn't factor in your growth as a new business and the potential of where it could be if your growth continues. Although the buyer won't care how much work went into making it or how much money you've personally invested at this point, those things matter to you. And, ultimately, you're the one who gets to decide if you sell or not. Instead of a 3x multiple, I've sold several businesses for 8x-10x and even one for 15x!

Figure out a price you're happy with and expect that you likely will get less. That's ok - especially if this is your first sale. The point is, you've got to start somewhere with your asking price and you'll likely negotiate a little with the buyer.

Finding a Buyer

Next, you'll need to find a buyer. I would, personally, avoid selling to family and friends unless you have a track record of doing business with them. The fact is that 90% of startups fail and, when they take it over, it might not perform as well as it did with you.

If your asking price is high, you may want to go through a brokerage. They can find buyers with big budgets who can pay millions for the right product. If you go this route, though, you need to have your act together. You need revenue to back up your valuation, proven tractions, tons of customers, and some secret sauce no one else has.

If your app isn't going to sell for millions and you're in the $200k or less range, you could have some great luck on platforms like Flippa and Empire Flippers. These are marketplaces for selling websites - including SaaS apps. There are engaged buyers and, if you're dedicated to the process and answering their questions, you can generally find a buyer this way.

Paying for a premium placement - usually like $100 - is worth it since it gets you in front of more buyers and can help drive up the price of the auction.

Negotiating a Deal

Once you find a buyer, they will likely want to negotiate a price with you. If you are selling in an auction format, you could accept their offer and cancel the auction. It's good to always consider your room to negotiate. If you are toward the end of your listing and you aren't getting your asking price - is their offer enough to make you happy? If you've just listed and already have several interested buyers, do you think you could get more if you wait?

When you're negotiating a deal, start with a realistic number, but also a little crazy. You always want to present an opportunity for them to take the first price you give them and get a payout you are really happy with. Chances are, they won't take it, but at least you tried. Maybe their counteroffer will still be more than you expected.

Here's an example of how a deal might go down. Your app is doing $10k per month and has done $80k total in the past year. You calculate that a fair price would be $240k, but with your current growth, you think you'll do that in the next 12 months. So you decide to list it for $500k. That would be 2 years worth of revenue upfront with no risk of new competitors, regulations, etc taking you off course.

You find an interested buyer, but they can't justify the valuation. At $500k, with the current revenue, it would take 50 months to make that back before they saw a profit. They counter with $300k and you accept.

Sometimes you might find yourself with an opportunity to get residual income from the deal as well. If you trust that the business acquiring your app will be around for a while, you could structure a deal where they pay less upfront, in this case, maybe $100k, and you get a portion of the revenue each month - say 15-20%.

The upside to a deal like this is that the app could be paying you for years to come and you could see way more money in the long run without having to work at building the business. The downside is that you risk the business going under, not doing well, the buyer stiffing you and refusing to pay, etc. When you do a deal like this, there should be some level of trust between yourself and the buyer - or at a minimum really strong contracts!

You'll get better at it the more deals you do, but, keep in mind that you never have to sell. It's up to you and you can walk away if the deal isn't right.

After you strike a deal with your buyer, you'll need to make the exchange of funds for assets. For these transactions, I always go through a platform with escrow if I don't already know the buyer so I know the money is good before I transfer anything over. There are scammers everywhere and you can never be too careful.

Once the money hits escrow, you can safely transfer over the login credentials to your hosting account, email and support apps, etc.

Then you get paid.

Congrats! You just turned an idea into an acquisition.

SaaS Acronyms Glossary

Whether you're building your first app or have done this a few times already, there are loads of acronyms you'll encounter on your journey. Here's a list of the ones I see the most with explanations of what they mean. Becoming familiar with this list will help you communicate better with potential partners, investors, employees, and customers.

AE - *Account Executive*: A salesperson responsible for serving the needs of existing customers and closing sales.

ACV - *Annual Contract Value*: Refers to the total value of a contract after it's executed including all fees for products, services, etc. divided by the number of years the contract covers.

API - *Application Programming Interface*: An interface of a software application that can be interacted with via 3rd-party scripts.

ARR - *Annual Run Rate*: This is a future prediction of the next 12 months of a business's revenue based on the previous reporting period.

ARPU - *Average Revenue Per User*: Total revenue during a given time period, divided by the total number of users during that period.

ASP - *Average Sale Price*: The price at which a product or service is typically sold.

ATS - *Applicant Tracking System*: Software used to track resumes and job applicants during the hiring process.

B2B - *Business-to-Business*: Businesses who sell to other businesses

B2C - *Business-to-Consumer*: Businesses who sell to consumers

BDR - *Business Development Representative*: A salesperson in charge of identifying, connecting with, and warming up leads.

BR - *Burn Rate*: The rate at which a business spends money over its income.

CAC - *Customer Acquisition Cost*: The total amount of money paid by a business, on average, to acquire one new customer.

CDP - *Customer Data Platform*: A software platform that functions as a consistent, unified customer database that is accessible by other systems.

COB - *Close of Business*: Refers to the end of the day when the business hours are over.

CPC - *Cost-per-click*: In paid advertising, the advertiser pays for each click on their ad during a campaign.

CPM - *Cost-per-mille(1,000)*: In paid advertising, this is the cost paid by the advertiser for every 1,000 impressions of an ad.

CR - *Conversion Rate*: The percentage of people who took an action compared to the total number of people who were presented with the opportunity.

CMRR - *Committed monthly recurring revenue*: Similar to monthly recurring revenue, but factors in new accounts in the current month and accounts for churn.

CRM – *Customer Relationship Management*: A software system designed to track the customer journey from sales through support.

D2C/DTC - *Direct-to-consumer*: Refers to selling products directly to consumers, bypassing any 3rd parties (retailers, distributors, etc).

EOD - *End of Day*: Refers to the end of someone's workday.

ERP - *Enterprise Resource Planning*: A process of structuring technologies and software used by a company to manage and integrate their core business processes.

GDPR - *General Data Protection Regulation*: A regulation in the European Union addressing data protection and privacy as well as personal data transferred outside the EU.

HIPAA - *Health Insurance Portability and Accountability Act of 1996*: United States federal statute designed to provide privacy standards and protect patient's healthcare data.

ICP – *Ideal Customer Profile*: A description of your ideal customer

KPI – *Key Performance Indicator*: A specific metric use by a company to gauge the efficacy of marketing and sales efforts within the company.

LTV - Customer *Lifetime Value*: The total amount a customer will pay a business over the lifetime of their account.

MQL - *Marketing Qualified Lead*: A lead that has been vetted by marketing and is deemed ready to be vetted by sales.

MRR - *Monthly recurring revenue*: The amount of revenue a business makes from subscriptions or every month.

MSA - *Master Service Agreement*: A contract between two businesses detailing the services rendered and money exchanged during the relationship.

MTD - *Month-to-date*: Use to specify a timeframe, generally in reporting, that includes all days from the 1st of the current month through today.

LTV - *Lifetime Value*: This is the average total amount of revenue made from a customer from the time they sign up until the time they close their account.

NPS - *Net Promoter Score*: A score representing a customer's sentiment around their experience with a business. Generally on a scale from 1 to 10.

OOO - *Out of Office*: Use to refer to someone being on vacation or done with work for the day. OOO replies are automated responses from someone's email when they are away.

P&L - *Profit and Loss Statement*: This document, generally prepared by an accountant, details the total profit and loss of a business over a given timeframe.

PCI Compliance- *Payment Card Industry Compliance*: A set of standards imposed by credit card companies to help ensure the security of credit card transactions.

PHI - *Protected Health Information*: Any individually identifiable health information such as demographic data, medical history, test results, etc.

POC - *Proof of Concept*: A trial run of an idea to determine if it's a viable business concept.

PQL - *Product Qualified Lead*: A customer who has received value from trying a product during a free trial or evaluation period.

RFP - *Request for Proposal*: A document detailing what a client needs to be done, inviting businesses to submit proposals to be considered for the project.

ROI - *Return on Investment*: The amount of profit earned from an investment of capital.

SaaS - *Software as a Service*: Software sales model in which the customer pays on a monthly or annual basis for access to software generally hosted in the cloud.

SAL - *Sales Accepted Lead*: A lead that has been accepted by sales as a verified lead and meets the previously determined criteria for qualification.

SDR - *Sales Development Representative*: A salesperson in charge of qualifying potential customers from inbound leads.

SE - *Sales Engineer*: A salesperson who facilitates the sales process for technologically or scientifically advanced products.

SEO - *Search Engine Optimization*: The process of tailoring your website's code structure and content to be easily identified and indexed by search engines.

SEM - *Search Engine Marketing*: A form of marketing centered around increasing a website's visibility and rankings on search engines.

SKO - *Sales Kick-off*: A meeting in which sales leaders get the sales team all on the same page. Generally held once per year or once per quarter.

SLA - *Service Level Agreement*: A contract between a business and a service provider stipulating required uptime for the service and penalties to the provider for downtime in service based on severity and length.

SMB - *Small and medium-sized businesses*: Businesses having less than 100 employees and between $5-10M in annual revenue.

SOC 2 - *Service Organization Control 2*: An auditing process that ensures software providers you work with are securing customer data effectively.

SOW - *Statement of Work*: A document detailing the full scope of a project, the time needed to complete it, and associated costs.

SQL - *Sales Qualified Lead*: A lead that has been vetted by both marketing and sales and is deemed ready for the next stage of business.

TAM - *Total Addressable Market*: The total amount of money you can make selling what you're selling based on market demand.

TCO - *Total Cost of Ownership*: A calculation that determines the total costs of a product or service throughout its lifecycle.

TCV - *Total Contract Value*: Refers to the total value of a contract after it's executed including all fees for products, services, etc.

UI - *User Interface*: The buttons, text, and inputs that a user interacts with when using a piece of software

UX - *User Experience*: The overall experience and ease of use when users use a piece of software.

YTD - *Year-to-date*: Use to specify a timeframe, generally in reporting, that includes all days from Jan 1 of the current year through today.

Resource Links

Trello
Task Management Software
https://trello.com/

PivotalTracker
Project Management Software
https://www.pivotaltracker.com/

Google Calendar
Calendar App
https://calendar.google.com/

Hootsuite
Social Media Automation
https://www.hootsuite.com/

LinkedIn
Social Network
https://www.linkedin.com/

LinkedIn Sales Navigator

Lead Generation Add-On

https://business.linkedin.com/sales-solutions/sales-navigator

Zoom

Video Conferencing Software

https://zoom.us

GoDaddy

Domain Registrar

https://www.godaddy.com

NameCheap

Domain Registrar

https://www.namecheap.com

Fiverr

Freelancer Marketplace

https://www.fiverr.com

Design Pickle

Unlimited Graphic Design

https://designpickle.com

Google Analytics

Website Analytics

https://marketingplatform.google.com/about/

Express

Node.js Web Application Framework

https://expressjs.com

Symfony
PHP Web Application Framework
https://symfony.com

Laravel
PHP Web Application Framework
https://laravel.com

Laracasts
Laravel Tutorial Videos
https://laracasts.com

Django
Python Web Application Framework
https://www.djangoproject.com

Bubble
No-Code Web Application Builder
http://bubble.io

Wavemaker
Low-code Web Application Builder
https://www.wavemaker.com

Journal of Neuroscience
Scientific Journal
https://www.jneurosci.org

Verblio
Hire content writers
https://www.verblio.com

WordPress

Open-source CMS

https://wordpress.com

Flywheel

Managed WordPress Hosting Service

https://getflywheel.com

Shopify

E-commerce Storefront Builder

https://www.shopify.com

Shopify App Marketplace

Shopify MicroSaaS extensions

https://apps.shopify.com

BigCommerce

E-commerce Storefront Builder

https://www.bigcommerce.ca

BigCommerce App Marketplace

BigCommerce MicroSaaS Extensions

https://www.bigcommerce.com/apps/

Salesforce

Enterprise CRM Tool

https://www.salesforce.com

Salesforce AppExchange

Salesforce MicroSaaS Extensions

https://appexchange.salesforce.com

Quora
Forum to ask and answer questions
https://www.quora.com

PayWhirl
Recurring Payments Platform
https://app.paywhirl.com

Sendlio
Marketing Automation Platform
https://www.sendlio.com

Growbots
Outbound sales platform
https://www.growbots.com

Flippa
Marketplace to Sell Websites
https://flippa.com

Empire Flippers
Website Brokers
https://empireflippers.com

Made in the USA
Columbia, SC
10 July 2021